Contents

Introduction

On 2 April 1982, after having declared that the diplomatic channels for discussions were closed, Argentina invaded and occupied the Falkland Islands, a British dependency with a population whose distinctive way of life stretches back nearly 150 years. Reporting the invasion to the House of Commons on 3 April, Britain's Prime Minister, Mrs Margaret Thatcher, said: 'I must tell the House that the Falkland Islands and their Dependencies remain British territory. No aggression and no invasion can alter that simple fact. It is the Government's objective to see that the Islands are freed from occupation and are returned to British administration at the earliest possible moment.'

The collection of documents in this pamphlet, together with a short account of the Falklands crisis, is designed to show the development of British policy in response to Argentina's invasion and subsequent refusal to withdraw its forces from the Islands in compliance with a mandatory resolution of the United Nations Security Council; the support Britain gave to the United States and other intermediaries in their efforts to promote a negotiated settlement of the dispute; and how, after Argentina had rejected all such attempts, Britain, in exercise of its right of self-defence, was compelled to use force to restore British administration to the Islands and secure the freedom of the Islanders to determine their own future.

The Crisis

Although Argentina claims sovereignty over the Falkland Islands on the ground that it has succeeded to rights claimed by Spain in the eighteenth century, the British title to the Islands is derived from early settlement reinforced by formal claims in the name of the Crown in the eighteenth century and completed by effective possession, occupation and administration for nearly 150 years. The exercise of sovereignty by Britain has consistently been shown to accord with the freely expressed wishes of the Falkland Islanders, who form the Islands' permanent population; the Islanders have repeatedly emphasised their wish to retain the link with Britain and not to become independent or associated with any other country.

Since 1965 various attempts have been made by Britain and Argentina to deal with the issue through negotiation, the most recent round of talks taking place in New York in February 1982.[1] These talks were held on the firm understanding that they were without prejudice to either side's position regarding sovereignty and Britain emphasised that any agreement had to be acceptable to the Islanders. During the discussions both sides considered an Argentine proposal that a negotiating commission at ministerial level should be created in order to speed up negotiations. In response Britain pointed out that the proposal required careful consideration and promised a reply as soon as possible. In a joint communiqué issued at the end of the meeting both countries reaffirmed their resolve to find a solution to the sovereignty dispute (see p 17). Within hours of issuing the communiqué, however, the Argentine Government published a statement in which it reserved the right to choose freely the procedure which best accorded with its interests.

The Argentine Invasion

Relations between Britain and Argentina deteriorated during March when a large group of workmen, sent on a commercial contract to dismantle a disused whaling station, landed in the British territory of South Georgia[2] without seeking the authorisation they had been told they would require from the British authorities. Although the Argentine ship later departed, a dozen or so men remained and on 25 March a supply ship made further deliveries to them. In an effort to ease the tension, Britain made it clear that if the party requested proper authorisation it could be given retrospectively. On 26 March Argentina said that it would give all necessary protection to the men and two days later, restating its claim to the Falkland Islands and Dependencies, rejected Britain's proposal to regularise the situation.

In a further endeavour to reach a peaceful settlement, the British Government proposed on 31 March that a special emissary should be sent to Buenos Aires for discussions. On the same day Britain received information that a large Argentine fleet was heading for the Falkland Islands. That evening, the Prime Minister, Mrs Margaret Thatcher, contacted the United States President, Mr Ronald Reagan, requesting him to

---

[1] *For further information on the history of the dispute and recent negotiations, see COI reference documents* The Falkland Islands and Dependencies, *No 152/82 (Revised), and* Falkland Islands: Britain's Search for a Negotiated Settlement *No 170/82.*

[2] *South Georgia and the South Sandwich Islands are British dependent territories legally distinct from the Falkland Islands. For convenience they are administered by the Falkland Islands Government which is empowered to legislate for them.*

2

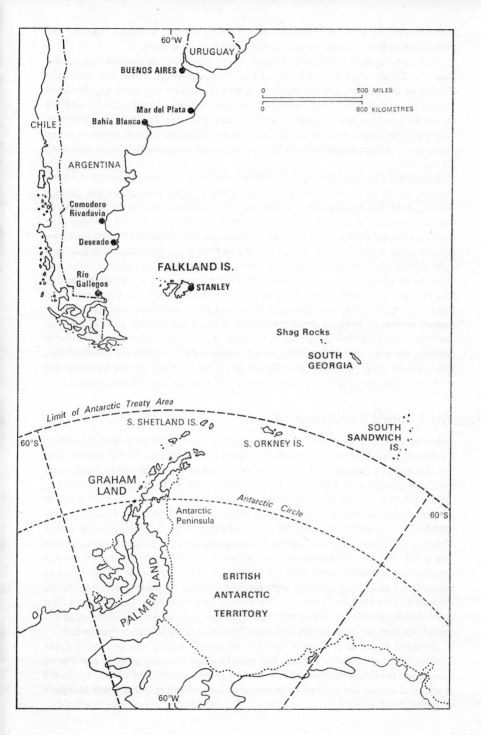

60°W

URUGUAY

BUENOS AIRES

Mar del Plata

Bahía Blanca

CHILE

ARGENTINA

**Comodoro
Rivadavia**

Deseado

**Río
Gallegos**

FALKLAND IS.

STANLEY

0   500 MILES

0   800 KILOMETRES

Shag Rocks

**SOUTH
GEORGIA**

Limit of Antarctic Treaty Area

S. SHETLAND IS.

60°S

S. ORKNEY IS.

**SOUTH
SANDWICH
IS.**

**GRAHAM
LAND**

Antarctic   Circle

Antarctic
Peninsula

60°S

PALMER LAND

BRITISH

ANTARCTIC

TERRITORY

60°W

3

intervene directly with the President of Argentina, General Leopoldo Galtieri, and promising that Britain would take no action to escalate the dispute.

On 1 April the Argentine Foreign Minister, Señor Nicanor Costa Mendez, rejected the idea of a British emissary and informed the British Ambassador that the diplomatic channel as a means of settling the dispute was closed. On the same day President Reagan in a telephone conversation with President Galtieri urged restraint, and the United Nations Secretary-General, Señor Pérez de Cuellar, met the British and Argentine Permanent Representatives to the United Nations and asked them to refrain from the threat or use of force. Señor Pérez de Cuellar also issued two press statements appealing for restraint.

During the afternoon of 1 April, the British Permanent Representative, Sir Anthony Parsons, called for an emergency meeting of the Security Council. At the Council meeting, held that evening, Sir Anthony said that there was strong evidence that an Argentine invasion of the Falkland Islands would take place on 2 April and requested the Council to call on Argentina to refrain from the use of force (see p 19). The Argentine representative, Señor Eduardo Roca, claimed that there was a British threat to use force against Argentina's territory leaving it no alternative but to adopt the necessary measures to ensure its self-defence. Argentina, said Señor Roca, was ready to negotiate provided that Britain made a prior recognition of Argentine sovereignty over the Islands. The President, Mr Kamanda wa Kamanda, then read out a statement on behalf of the Council expressing concern about the tension in the South Atlantic and calling upon the British and Argentine Governments to refrain from the use or threat of force and to continue the search for a diplomatic solution (see p 23). Sir Anthony promised that Britain would comply with the Council's call (see p 24) but the Argentine representative remained silent. On 2 April Argentina invaded and occupied the Falkland Islands.

Security Council Resolution 502

Following another request from Britain, the Security Council met on 2 April. Describing the invasion as a 'blatant violation of the United Nations Charter and of international law', Sir Anthony Parsons said that it was an attempt to impose by force a foreign and unwanted control over 1,800 people who had chosen in fair and free elections to maintain their links with Britain and the British way of life. He also read out a British draft resolution demanding the immediate withdrawal of all Argentine forces from the Islands and a cessation of hostilities, and calling upon the two countries to seek a diplomatic solution to their difficulties in conformity with the United Nations Charter (see p 25). The Argentine representative, Señor Roca, said that a situation of tension and injustice had been ended which, he alleged, had been a constant disturbance to international peace and security; although the interests of Britain were negotiable, sovereignty over the Islands was not. The French, Irish, Australian, Canadian and New Zealand representatives pointed out that Argentina had deliberately disregarded the appeals for restraint made by the Secretary-General and the Council's President.

Speaking to the Council on 3 April the Argentine Foreign Minister, Señor Costa Mendez, said that Argentina's action had ended a classic colonial problem and that no provision of the United Nations Charter could legalise a situation which had originated in wrongful acts carried out before its adoption. Responding to Señor Costa Mendez's allegation that the recent tension was due to Britain's sending of warships to intimidate

Argentina, Sir Anthony Parsons said that the incident in South Georgia was a relative triviality which Britain had had no intention of resolving by force. It could not justify the armed invasion of an inhabited group of islands 1,300 km (800 miles) away. The Falkland Islanders were entitled to the protection of international law and to have their freely expressed wishes respected. He also pointed out that the use of force to resolve situations originating before the adoption of the Charter would make the world an infinitely more dangerous place (see p 31).

The Security Council adopted the British draft resolution, under chapter 7 of the United Nations Charter, thereby making it mandatory. Security Council resolution 502 (see p 34) was supported by Britain, the United States, France, the Irish Republic, Japan, Zaïre, Togo, Uganda, Guyana and Jordan. The Soviet Union, the People's Republic of China, Poland and Spain abstained while Panama voted against. Argentina refused to comply with the resolution. On the same day Argentine forces occupied the island of South Georgia.

Britain's Response

In a special debate in the House of Commons on 3 April, the Prime Minister, Mrs Margaret Thatcher, condemned Argentina's unprovoked and illegal aggression and emphasised the Government's determination to free the Islands from occupation and to return them to British administration at the earliest possible moment (see p 26). Britain had no doubt about its sovereignty or of the unequivocal wishes of the Falkland Islanders. For 15 years, she pointed out, successive British Governments had made it clear to Argentina that the Islanders' wishes were paramount and that there could be no change in sovereignty without their consent and that of the British Parliament.

Britain's inherent right of self-defence recognised by Article 51 of the United Nations Charter (see p 94) would have justified the adoption of a purely military policy for settling the crisis. From the outset, however, the Government directed major efforts towards achieving the peaceful implementation of resolution 502. Although immediate measures were taken to dispatch a naval task force to the South Atlantic, the first ships leaving Britain on 5 April, this, as the Foreign and Commonwealth Secretary, Mr Francis Pym, explained in the House of Commons on 7 April (see p 35), represented part of a policy of bringing increasing pressure on Argentina with a view to convincing it that withdrawal from the Islands and a negotiated settlement constituted the only legal and acceptable approach in the dispute and the only one which was in Argentina's own interests. The preservation of peace depended on the international community supporting the principle of self-determination and punishing those who violated it. If it did not, then the world would become an even more dangerous place. Before the task force's arrival in the South Atlantic, there would be time to do everything possible to solve the problem without further fighting. Mr Pym also made it clear that Britain was prepared to use force in exercise of its right of self-defence if these efforts failed. Not to be prepared to do this, he told the House on 29 April (see p 48), would be irresponsible since it was 'in the interests of the whole free world that the rule of law should be upheld and that aggression should not prevail'.

Britain also sought to influence Argentina through economic and diplomatic pressure. In addition to severing diplomatic relations, the Government froze all Argentine financial assets held in Britain, banned imports from Argentina, suspended new export credit cover, and banned the export to Argentina of arms and other military equipment. Furthermore, Britain urged its allies and friends to adopt similar measures and sought the widest international condemnation of Argentina's action. In so doing the Government emphasised that it was in the interests of the whole world that Argentina should fulfil its legal obligations under the mandatory United Nations resolution.

International Reaction

In addition to the United Nations Security Council, several other international organisations and many governments deplored the Argentine invasion.

On 2 April European Community foreign ministers issued a declaration condemning Argentina and urgently appealing to it to withdraw its forces from the Islands. Eight days later the foreign ministers announced an embargo on arms and military equipment for Argentina and on 16 April banned imports from Argentina. On 20 April they reaffirmed their solidarity with Britain, confirmed their desire for full implementation of resolution 502, called for a peaceful solution to the crisis and expressed strong support for the efforts of the United States Secretary of State, Mr Alexander Haig, to encourage a settlement (see p 7). Two days later the European Parliament approved by 203 votes to 28 a resolution condemning the invasion and backing the United Nations demand for the withdrawal of all Argentine forces. On 7 April the Council of Europe also supported resolution 502 and reaffirmed the commitment of its member states to settle disputes by peaceful means.

Major support for Britain also came from members of the Commonwealth. On 2 April the Commonwealth Secretary-General, Mr Shridath Ramphal, urged all member states to stand by Britain and, speaking in Port of Spain, Trinidad and Tobago, on 6 April, condemned the invasion and called for Argentine withdrawal. What was at stake, he emphasised, was 'the seizure of territory by force, the attempt to change long-established boundaries otherwise than by peaceful means and the repudiation of the principle of self-determination'.

At a special meeting of the North Atlantic Council of the North Atlantic Treaty Organisation (NATO), held on 2 April, member states expressed deep concern about the dispute and requested both parties to refrain from the use or threat of force. Britain's NATO allies subsequently condemned the Argentine use of force.

In addition to European Community member states, some other countries took diplomatic or economic sanctions against Argentina. New Zealand broke off diplomatic relations with Argentina and several countries recalled their ambassadors from Buenos Aires. States which undertook not to supply arms to Argentina included the United States, Australia, Canada, New Zealand, Austria and Switzerland. Australia, Canada and New Zealand also banned imports from Argentina and stopped export credits.

While most Latin American countries supported Argentina's position on sovereignty, few endorsed the use of force. On 13 April the Organisation of American States expressed the hope that a rapid peaceful solution could be found to the dispute and offered to co-operate in peace efforts. On 28 April the Organisation, while supporting Argentina's claim to sovereignty and deploring the European Community's economic sanctions against Argentina, urged both sides to resume negotiations aimed at a peaceful settlement of the conflict, bearing in mind the interests of the Islanders.

The Search for a Negotiated Solution

In its diplomatic efforts to achieve a solution, Britain could have simply demanded, as it was entitled to do under resolution 502, the total withdrawal of the aggressor and the restoration of the *status quo*. The Government, however, was prepared to discuss possible arrangements for supervising the withdrawal and for a degree of international involvement in the administration of the Islands. At the same time, however, it remained resolute in its adherence to certain principles, notably the need to uphold international law through the ending of the Argentine aggression and the implementation of resolution 502, and freedom for the Falkland Islanders to participate, through their elected representatives, in the running of their own affairs and to express their wishes about the Islands' future. In addition, while ready to enter negotiations for a long-term settlement of the dispute, the Government stated that it was only prepared to do so on condition that there was no attempt to predetermine or prejudge the outcome, whether on sovereignty or other matters.

United States Initiative

The first diplomatic attempt to secure an interim settlement, based on resolution 502, was made by the then United States Secretary of State, Mr Alexander Haig, with the full support of the British Government. At the same time Britain was involved in constant activity at the United Nations where Sir Anthony Parsons had many discussions with the Secretary-General, Señor Pérez de Cuellar.

In April Mr Haig visited London and Buenos Aires twice in a bid to obtain a settlement. On 21 April, announcing a forthcoming visit to Washington for discussions with Mr Haig, Mr Pym told the House of Commons that any satisfactory negotiation had to deal with arrangements for Argentine withdrawal, the nature of any interim administration of the Islands, and the framework for negotiations on a long-term solution to the dispute.

On his arrival in Washington on 22 April Mr Pym said that, while Britain would do everything possible to find a peaceful solution, there were real difficulties and obstacles. Following discussions with Mr Haig, he met the Senate Foreign Relations Committee to present the British case regarding the dispute. Nearly all the Senators expressed support for Britain and at the end of the meeting the Committee's Chairman, Senator Charles Percy, told a press conference that, if Argentina's use of force were successful, a damaging precedent would have been set. He also expressed the view that the people of the United States solidly supported Britain. On 29 April the Senate adopted, by 79 votes to 1, a resolution declaring that the United States could not remain neutral and should work to achieve a full withdrawal of Argentine forces. On 4 May the House of Representatives urged Argentina to withdraw and called for full diplomatic support for Britain.

After Mr Pym's return to Britain, Mr Haig had further talks in Washington with the Argentine Foreign Minister, Señor Costa Mendez, but no progress was made. On 26 April, addressing a conference of the Organisation of American States, Mr Haig said that the Organisation and the world community had made the judgment long ago that force should not be used to solve international disputes. In the current conflict the surest guide to a peaceful settlement was to be found in resolution 502, which formed 'the indispensable basis for a solution'. The United States, explained Mr Haig, had

7

offered its assistance to both Britain and Argentina and he had pursued 'the possibilities of averting wider conflict and a framework for a peaceful settlement'.

Negotiations foundered because of Argentina's refusal to accept compromise proposals elaborated by Mr Haig. These involved the withdrawal of both Argentine and British forces, the ending of economic sanctions, the establishment of a British-United States-Argentine interim authority to maintain the agreement, continuation of the traditional local administration with Argentine participation, procedures for encouraging co-operation in the development of the Islands, and a framework for negotiations on a final settlement taking account of the interests of both sides and the wishes of the inhabitants. Although these proposals presented certain difficulties, Britain expressed willingness to consider them but Argentina rejected them by demanding an immediate assurance of eventual sovereignty or an immediate *de facto* role in governing the Islands which would lead to sovereignty.

Following the Argentine refusal to compromise, President Reagan ordered on 30 April the suspension of all military exports to Argentina, the withholding of certification of Argentine eligibility for military sales and the suspension of new Export-Import Bank credits and guarantees and of commodity credit guarantees. In addition, Mr Reagan promised a positive response to requests from Britain for material support for its forces.

New Peace Proposals

After the breakdown of Mr Haig's initiative, Mr Pym visited Washington and New York early in May for talks with Mr Haig and Señor Pérez de Cuellar. During these, he emphasised Britain's concern to secure the implementation of resolution 502 and its readiness to consider any ideas which would achieve an Argentine withdrawal followed by negotiations on a long-term solution without prejudice to basic principles. Discussions were focused on proposals originally advanced by President Belaúnde Terry of Peru and subsequently modified in consultations between him and Mr Haig. On 6 May Britain accepted interim arrangements providing for a complete and supervised withdrawal of Argentine forces from the Islands matched by corresponding withdrawal of British forces; an immediate ceasefire following Argentine agreement to withdraw; the appointment of a small group of countries acceptable to both sides who would supervise withdrawal, undertake the interim administration in consultation with the Islanders' elected representatives and assist in negotiating a definite agreement on the status of the Islands without prejudice to Britain's own principles or the wishes of the Islanders; and the suspension of existing exclusion zones and the lifting of economic sanctions. These proposals, which did not prejudice negotiations for a long-term settlement, but simply acknowledged the differences between the parties over the Islands, were rejected by the Argentine Government, which continued to insist that a transfer of sovereignty should be the pre-condition of negotiations for a final settlement.

UN Secretary-General's Initiative

The next attempt to achieve a peaceful settlement was undertaken by Señor Pérez de Cuellar who, in an *aide-mémoire* given to Britain and Argentina on 2 May, put forward a number of proposals intended to be without prejudice to the rights, claims or positions of either party. They included the withdrawal by an agreed date of Argentine troops from the Islands and of British forces from the area around the Falkland Islands; negotiations by both Governments to seek a diplomatic solution to their differences by an agreed date; the rescinding by both sides of blockades and exclusion zones and the ending of hostilities; the ending of all economic sanctions; and transitional arrangements under which these measures would be supervised and interim requirements met (see p 74). On 6 May Britain replied stating that resolution 502 had to be implemented without delay and that a ceasefire had to be unambiguously linked to the commencement of Argentine withdrawal within a fixed number of days.

From 7 May Señor Pérez de Cuellar had some 30 separate meetings with both sides. During these negotiations, as in earlier ones, Britain made repeated efforts to establish whether Argentina was willing to be sufficiently flexible to make a reasonable interim agreement possible. In a report made to the Security Council on 21 May (see p 73), Señor Pérez de Cuellar said that in his judgment agreement had been obtained on a number of points but that crucial differences remained regarding the interim administration, the withdrawal of forces and the geographical area to be covered by the terms of the interim agreement; there was also disagreement on provisions for the extension of the time to be allowed for the completion of negotiations and the related duration of the interim administration.

Britain's Final Proposals

On 17 May Britain presented its final proposals to Señor Pérez de Cuellar in the form of a draft interim agreement between the British and Argentine Governments (see p 59). This provided among other things for complete Argentine withdrawal from the Islands within 14 days; a withdrawal of all British and Argentine armed forces to at least 150 nautical miles radius from the Islands (also within 14 days); international verification of the withdrawals; the lifting of exclusion zones; and the lifting of economic sanctions against Argentina. A United Nations Administrator was to administer the government of the Islands in conformity with traditional laws and practices and in consultation with the Legislative and Executive Councils, the Islanders' representative institutions developed in accordance with the terms of Article 73 of the United Nations Charter (see p 95). Britain also expressed its readiness to enter into negotiations under the auspices of the United Nations Secretary-General for a peaceful settlement of the dispute and to seek completion of the negotiations by 31 December 1982 provided that no outcome should be either excluded or pre-determined.

In its reply, received by Britain on 19 May, Argentina wanted the withdrawal of forces to be completed in 30 days followed by their return to their normal bases and areas of operation. The administration of the Islands was to be the exclusive responsibility of the United Nations (though with Argentine and British observers present) which would have been free to appoint advisers in equal numbers from the small Argentine population and the much larger population of British origin. Argentina also wanted free access for its nationals to the Islands with respect to residence, work and property, and opposed the British view that the United Nations Administrator should exercise his powers in conformity with the laws and practices traditionally observed in the Islands. As for negotiations concerning the Islands' future, Argentina stated that these should be initiated without prejudice to the rights, claims and positions of the

9

two parties but would not accept an additional phrase stating that the outcome should not be prejudged. Argentina also resisted a provision in the British draft designed to ensure that the interim arrangements should remain in place until a definitive agreement about the future of the Islands could be implemented.

Britain was unable to accept Argentina's response because it included entirely unbalanced provisions regarding withdrawal. Had both sides returned their forces to their normal bases, Argentina's would have been 640 km (400 miles) away from the Islands and the British 12,900 km (8,000 miles) away with nothing to prevent the return of Argentine troops. Equally unsatisfactory features of the Argentine response were the destruction of the previous democratic structures of government on the Islands, opportunities for Argentina to change the character of the Islands in its favour and terms of reference for long-term negotiations which led in only one direction.

On 20 May the Prime Minister told the House of Commons that Britain's proposals represented a responsible effort to find a peaceful solution to the conflict and that Argentina had totally rejected these and all previous proposals designed to achieve a settlement (see p 67).

On 21 May, the United Nations Secretary-General reported to the Security Council and gave a detailed account of his attempt to obtain an agreement between Britain and Argentina (see p 73). In response Sir Anthony Parsons said that Argentina had in practice rejected resolution 502 by reinforcing its forces on the Islands and imposing its military government in place of democratic rule. In these circumstances Britain had no choice but to exercise its right of self-defence under Article 51 of the Charter (see p 94).

Further Efforts

On 26 May the Security Council unanimously passed resolution 505 (see p 86) reaffirming resolution 502 and requesting the Secretary-General to undertake a renewed mission of good offices and urging both parties to co-operate fully with a view to ending the hostilities in and around the Islands. The resolution requested the Secretary-General 'to enter into contact immediately with the parties with a view to negotiating mutually acceptable terms for a ceasefire, including, if necessary, arrangements for the dispatch of United Nations observers to monitor compliance with the terms of the ceasefire', and 'to submit an interim report to the Security Council as soon as possible and in any case not later than seven days after the adoption of this resolution'. While supporting the resolution and promising full co-operation with the Secretary-General, Sir Anthony Parsons stressed that the only acceptable condition for a ceasefire was that it should be unequivocally linked with an immediate commencement of Argentine withdrawal (see p 87).

Reporting to the Security Council on 2 June, Señor Pérez de Cuellar said that on 26 May he had met separately the British and Argentine representatives and had requested them to provide within 24 hours a statement of the terms they considered acceptable for a ceasefire. Both Governments had complied but, although he had explored various approaches in seeking agreement, there was no possibility of a ceasefire mutually acceptable to both sides.

Paying tribute to the Secretary-General for his efforts, Sir Anthony Parsons told the Council on 2 June that Britain's position was that 'it would welcome a ceasefire which was inseparably linked to the commencement of the withdrawal of Argentine forces and to the completion of their withdrawal within a fixed period'. He made it plain that a ceasefire not linked to an Argentine withdrawal was inconsistent with resolution 502, and that the call for an unconditional ceasefire would leave Argentine forces in position (see p 88).

On 4 June the Security Council voted on a draft resolution requesting both parties to cease fire and to initiate, simultaneously with the ceasefire, the implementation of resolutions 502 and 505 in their entirety. Sponsored by Spain and Panama, the draft resolution received nine votes and there were four abstentions. Britain and the United States voted against.[1] Explaining Britain's opposition to the draft resolution, Sir Anthony Parsons said that it did not meet the criteria of an immediate ceasefire linked inseparably to the immediate and total withdrawal of Argentine forces from the Falkland Islands.

Military Developments

From the outset Britain made it clear that, while committed to a diplomatic solution, it would be prepared, if necessary, to use force to secure the withdrawal of the occupying troops, in accordance with Article 51 of the United Nations Charter. Britain's naval task force set sail in early April and comprised aircraft carriers, guided missile destroyers, frigates, assault ships with landing craft, and supporting vessels. A strong force of Royal Marine Commandos, and Sea Harrier aircraft and many anti-submarine and troop-carrying helicopters were also embarked. Ships from the Merchant Navy (including cruise liners) were also requisitioned to carry troops and supplies. More than a hundred Royal Navy and requisitioned ships were involved in the operation, and altogether over 28,000 servicemen and civilians, men and women, sailed with the task force.

After the dispatch of the task force, the Secretary of State for Defence, Mr John Nott, told the House of Commons on 7 April that a maritime exclusion zone would be established around the Islands in order to deny the Argentine forces means of re-inforcement and re-supply from the mainland (see p 38). On 12 April the zone came into force, the outer limit being a circle of 200 nautical miles radius from the centre of the Islands (latitude 51°40' South, longitude 59°30' West). Britain pointed out that any Argentine warships or naval auxiliaries found within the zone would be treated as hostile and liable to be attacked by British forces. At the same time it made clear that this measure was without prejudice to Britain's right to take whatever additional measures might be needed in exercise of the right of self-defence. On 23 April Britain informed the Argentine Government that 'any approach on the part of Argentine warships, including submarines, naval auxiliaries or military aircraft which could amount to a threat to interfere with the mission of the British forces in the South Atlantic will encounter the appropriate response' (see p 42).

Following the arrival of the task force in the area of the Falkland Islands, Britain announced that the maritime exclusion zone would become a total exclusion zone with effect from 30 April, and would be applicable to all ships and aircraft, whether military or civil, operating in support of Argentina's illegal occupation (see p 43).

---

[1] *After the vote the United States representative, Mrs Jeane Kirkpatrick, said that she had been instructed by her Government to report that were it possible to change its vote the United States would change it from a veto to an abstention.*

On 7 May Argentina was told that any of its warships or military aircraft more than 12 nautical miles from the Argentine coast would be treated as hostile and dealt with as appropriate (a move which was necessary because of the proximity of Argentine bases, the threat posed by Argentine carrier-borne aircraft and the ability of hostile forces to approach undetected in bad weather and at low level.)

South Georgia Landing

On 25 April British troops, supported by a number of warships, landed on South Georgia and quickly secured the surrender of the Argentine forces at Grytviken. During the first phase of the operation the Argentine submarine *Santa Fe* was attacked and disabled. With Grytviken having been taken a separate landing party deployed to Leith, and on 26 April the officer commanding the Argentine forces on South Georgia, Captain Alfredo Astiz, formally surrendered. About 180 prisoners were taken including 50 military reinforcements who were in the submarine. The minimum of force was used and no lives—Argentine or British—were lost during the operation itself.

Aerial and Naval Engagements

Following the declaration of the total exclusion zone, several naval and aerial military engagements took place between Argentine and British forces. From 1 May several attacks were made by Vulcan and Sea Harrier aircraft on the runway of Port Stanley airport in order to prevent landings by Argentine transport aircraft, and on the next day a naval bombardment of the airfield took place. The other main airfield, at Goose Green on East Falkland, was also attacked. On 1 May Argentine Mirage and Canberra aircraft operating from the mainland attacked British ships; these were repulsed by the task force's Sea Harriers, which shot down one Canberra and one Mirage.

Despite Britain's warning to Argentina on 23 April (see p 42), the Argentine cruiser, *General Belgrano*, escorted by two destroyers, was detected just outside the total exclusion zone by a British submarine on 2 May. This posed a threat to British ships, and the submarine torpedoed the cruiser which later sank. The two accompanying destroyers, however, were not attacked and were thus able to go to the cruiser's assistance, though they did not do so for several hours. (Nearly 800 of the cruiser's crew, which numbered some 1,100, were rescued.) On 3 May a British Sea King helicopter was fired on by an Argentine patrol craft which was then attacked and sunk by two Lynx helicopters. Both helicopters then came under attack from another Argentine vessel which was attacked and damaged by a Sea King missile. Before retiring the helicopters dropped survival equipment in the vicinity of the vessel.

On 4 May, HMS *Sheffield* was attacked by Argentine Super Etendard fighter aircraft which launched two Exocet missiles. Although one missile missed the ship, the other hit it amidships and, although it did not explode, caused a major fire. Attempts were made to extinguish the fire but after nearly four hours it spread out of control and the order was given to abandon ship. Some 20 men on board were killed and 24 injured. During further air operations conducted over the Islands on the same day, one Sea Harrier was shot down and the pilot killed.

Giving details of the early engagements, the Secretary of State for Defence, Mr John Nott, reminded the House of Commons on 4 May that the Government had made it clear

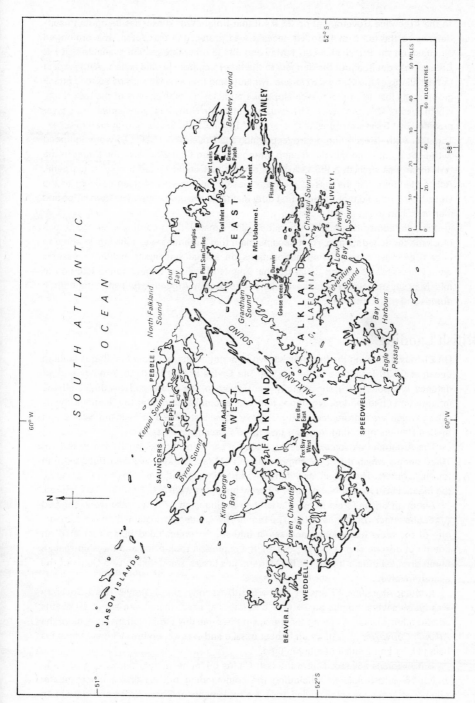

to the Argentine Government on 23 April that Britain would exercise its rights to self-defence to the full if this proved necessary to protect the task force. The prolonged air attack on the British ships on 1 May and all the other information available had left Britain in no doubt about the dangers to the task force from hostile action. With respect to the sinking of the *General Belgrano*, Mr Nott said that a heavily armed surface attack group was close to the total exclusion zone and closing on elements of the task force, which was only hours away. The cruiser, stated Mr Nott, had 'substantial fire power provided by 15 six-inch guns, with a range of 13 miles, and Seacat anti-aircraft missiles'. Together with its escorting destroyers, which the Government believed were equipped with Exocet anti-ship missiles having a range of more than 20 miles, 'the threat to the task force was such that the task force commander could ignore it only at his peril'. Acknowledging that the loss of life from these incidents was of deep concern to the House, Mr Nott said that Britain's first duty had to be the protection of its own ships and men who had to act in self-defence.

Periodic bombardments of Argentine military installations continued as the British blockade tightened its grip. As it became plain that Argentina was refusing to agree to interim arrangements pending negotiations on a final settlement, military pressures were increased. Naval and aerial bombardments of military targets continued, and in mid-May several raiding parties were landed to destroy Argentine fuel and ammunition dumps and military stores.

British Landing

On 21 May, following the final breakdown in negotiations, a major amphibious landing began at 03.20 local time in the area of San Carlos in East Falkland. Artillery and air defence weapons were successfully transferred to the shore and by 09.00 all the infantry units had landed. No opposition was encountered during the landings them-selves which were protected by Royal Navy vessels stationed in Falkland Sound and by Sea Harriers operating from the task force's aircraft carriers.

The Argentine air force, however, began a series of attacks on British vessels at 10.30 during which it lost 17 combat aircraft (Mirages, Skyhawks and Pucaras) and four helicopters. The British air defence was penetrated and five ships were damaged, the frigate HMS *Ardent* being sunk; 22 crew members were killed and 17 were injured.

Although British forces consolidated their positions on 22 May, there were renewed Argentine attacks on the next day. The frigate HMS *Antelope* sustained severe damage, one of the crew being killed and seven injured. An unexploded bomb remained on board but despite efforts to defuse it a large explosion took place and the ship sank, a bomb disposal officer losing his life. Argentina's losses amounted to two-thirds of the aircraft involved.

In other Argentine air attacks in the South Atlantic, the destroyer HMS *Coventry* was hit by several bombs on 25 May and later capsized; there were about 20 deaths and 20 other casualties among the crew. On the same day the Merchant Navy ship, the *Atlantic Conveyor*, was hit by an Exocet missile and was set on fire, 13 crew members being killed and a small number injured.

British forces advanced from the San Carlos bridgehead and, following a battle in which 16 British soldiers (including the commanding officer) and a much greater number of Argentine soldiers died, took the settlements of Goose Green and Darwin on

28 May. Over 900 prisoners were taken. In another and more northerly advance from the San Carlos bridgehead, other forces seized Douglas and Teal Inlet. By the beginning of June the high ground around Mount Kent, some 19 km (12 miles) from Stanley, had been occupied.

On 8 June some 50 British soldiers were killed when Argentine aircraft attacked two Royal Navy Fleet Auxiliary landing ships, the *Sir Galahad* and *Sir Tristram*, as they were about to land troops at Fitzroy. Further casualties occurred on 12 June when 13 crewmen were killed during an attack on HMS *Glamorgan*, which was providing naval support to land forces advancing on Stanley.

Following rapid advances by British troops across the island to capture high ground dominating the capital, Argentine defences were soon breached, and, following talks between the commander of the Argentine forces, General Mario Menendez, and emissaries of the commander of the British land forces, Major-General (now Sir) Jeremy Moore, on 14 June, General Menendez surrendered over 11,000 men, including those already in custody. Under the terms of the surrender the Argentine soldiers handed over their weapons and ammunition and Britain undertook to treat them in accordance with conditions set out in the 1949 Geneva Convention. The Argentine prisoners of war were later returned to Argentina on British ships although some 600 remained in custody pending an official cessation of hostilities.

On 15 June Britain sent notes to Argentina through the embassies of Switzerland and Brazil seeking confirmation of the total cessation of hostilities. In response Argentina stated on 18 June that a total cessation of hostilities would be achieved only if certain conditions were fulfilled, including the withdrawal of British forces from the Islands. In a letter to the President of the United Nations Security Council on 23 June, the British Permanent Representative, Sir Anthony Parsons, said that this condition was totally unacceptable to Britain and that its forces were there to defend the Islands and their people against further attacks and to help the Islanders repair the extensive damage caused by the Argentine invasion and occupation. Sir Anthony emphasised that the Islands were British territory with a British population and that there could, therefore, be no question of withdrawing British forces.

On 9 July a British message was sent to the Argentine Government via the Swiss Embassy in Buenos Aires noting that there had been no further hostilities in the South Atlantic since 14 June and that the Argentine Foreign Minister had stated on 5 July that there was a *de facto* ceasefire on the part of Argentina. It therefore proposed that the remaining prisoners of war in British hands should be returned to Argentina. Two days later the Argentine Government replied saying that 'in view of the present state of *de facto* cessation of hostilities' arrangements should be made for the prisoners' return. On 12 July Britain expressed satisfaction at Argentina's acceptance of the ending of active hostilities and said that the remaining 600 prisoners would be returned.

Repossession of Southern Thule

On 20 June British forces retook control of Southern Thule when a party of military personnel at an illegal Argentine navy research station surrendered. Southern Thule is a group of three small islands and forms part of the South Sandwich Islands which is British sovereign territory. The Argentine research station was set up without British authorisation at the end of 1976 and was maintained despite subsequent British protests. The surrender marked the final stage of the operation to free the Falkland Islands and Dependencies.

Restoration of British Administration

On 25 June the former Governor, Mr Rex Hunt, returned to the Islands as Civil Commissioner with responsibility for all matters relating to civil administration. The commander of British land forces was designated Military Commissioner with responsibility for defence and internal security, excluding the police.

Documents[1]

1. British-Argentine Joint Communiqué issued following talks in New York on 26 and 27 February 1982

The British and Argentine Governments held a meeting at ministerial level in New York on 26 and 27 February 1982 to discuss the Falkland Islands question within the negotiating framework referred to in the relevant resolutions of the United Nations General Assembly.

The British and Argentine delegations were led respectively by Mr Richard Luce, MP, Minister of State at the Foreign and Commonwealth Office in London, and Ambassador Enrique Ros, Under-Secretary of State at the Ministry of Foreign Affairs and Worship in Buenos Aires.

The meeting took place in a cordial and positive spirit. The two sides reaffirmed their resolve to find a solution to the sovereignty dispute and considered in detail an Argentine proposal for procedures to make better progress in this sense. They agreed to inform their Governments accordingly.

2. Negotiations with Argentina: Statement by the Minister of State for Foreign and Commonwealth Affairs, Mr Richard Luce, in the House of Commons on 3 March 1982

I met the Argentine Under-Secretary of State for Foreign Affairs for discussions on the Falkland Islands question on 26 and 27 February in New York. While we both agreed on the need to resolve the dispute and discussed future procedures, I made it clear that we had no doubts about British sovereignty, and that no solution could be agreed that was not acceptable to the Islanders and to the House....

---

[1] *Where necessary some documents have been edited for ease of reading and to keep repetition to a minimum, but no significant points have been omitted.*

3. South Georgia incident: Statement by the Secretary of State for Foreign and Commonwealth Affairs, Lord Carrington,[1] in the House of Lords on 30 March 1982

My Lords, as my noble friend Lord Trefgarne informed the House on 23 March, a group of Argentines, employed by a commercial contractor, Mr Davidoff, an Argentine citizen, landed at Leith Harbour on South Georgia on 19 March from an Argentine naval transport vessel. Mr Davidoff had been informed in advance of the need to seek the necessary permission from the British authorities at Grytviken to land and to carry out this salvage work. He conveyed to the British Embassy in Buenos Aires his intention to begin work in South Georgia but gave no indication that he would not follow the normal immigration procedures.

When the party arrived at Leith they did not seek the required documentation: and when requested by the base commander to proceed to Grytviken in order to do so, they failed to comply. Mr Davidoff's commercial contract is straightforward. But it does not absolve him or his employees from complying with normal immigration procedures. Subsequently, the majority of the Argentinian party and the Argentinian ship departed: but about a dozen men remained on shore.

We therefore made it clear to the Argentine Government that we regarded them as being present illegally on British territory, and sought their co-operation in arranging for their departure, pointing out however that their position could be regularised if they were to seek the necessary authorisation. Meanwhile, HMS *Endurance* was ordered to proceed to the area to be available to assist as necessary. She has been standing by since 24 March.

On 25 March an Argentine vessel delivered further equipment to the group ashore. The Argentine Foreign Minister has said that the Argentine party in South Georgia will be given the full protection of the Argentine Government. Argentine warships are in the area.

The situation which has thus arisen, while not of our seeking, is potentially dangerous. We have no doubts about British sovereignty over this Falkland Islands dependency as over the Falklands themselves.

We remain of the view that the unauthorised presence of Argentine citizens in British territory is not acceptable. We have no wish to stand in the way of a normal commercial salvage contract, but the position of those carrying it out must be properly authorised. Further escalation of this dispute is in no one's interest. In these circumstances it is clearly right to pursue a diplomatic solution of this problem. This we are doing. I hope that the Argentine Government will take the same view. Meanwhile, the question of security in the Falklands area is being reviewed, although the House will understand that I prefer to say nothing in public about our precautionary measures. I can, however, inform the House that HMS *Endurance* will remain on station as long as is necessary.

---

[1] *Lord Carrington resigned as Foreign and Commonwealth Secretary on 5 April 1982.*

4. Statement by Britain's Permanent Representative to the United Nations, Sir Anthony Parsons, on 1 April 1982 requesting the Security Council to call upon Argentina to refrain from the use or threat of force in the South Atlantic

... As members of the Council will be aware, there have been differences for many years between my Government and the Government of the Republic of Argentina concerning the Falkland Islands. My Government has asked for this emergency meeting of the Council because it now has reason to believe that the Government of Argentina is planning to attempt to invade these islands.

The Falklands are situated in the South Atlantic, some 770 km north-east of Cape Horn. They have a population of about 1,900 people. These are people of mainly British origin, most of whom have been born there to families which have lived there for generations. There is no significant Argentine element in the population. The United Kingdom has exercised sovereignty over the Falkland Islands since early in the nineteenth century and continues to do so today.

For several years the affairs of the Falklands have been discussed by the General Assembly. The Falklands are one of those territories about which the United Kingdom reports to the United Nations under Article 73 (e) of the Charter. At the most recent session of the General Assembly, a decision was adopted to the effect that the Committee of 24[1] should keep the situation in the territory under review. The Assembly has not adopted a resolution on the subject for several years but has contented itself with taking note of developments.

My Government and the Government of Argentina have held a series of meetings to discuss the situation in the Falkland Islands. In these meetings, elected representatives of the local population have regularly taken part. Reports have been submitted to the General Assembly about these meetings, most recently in a note dated 1 April 1981. In this note, it is stated that: 'Both delegations . . . agreed that this question should be examined in further negotiations at an early date.'

Such discussions did in fact continue, most recently in New York at the end of February. Representatives of the two Governments confirmed on that occasion their wish to continue their discussions within the negotiating framework referred to in the relevant resolutions of the General Assembly. But, regrettably, the Argentine Government appears to have decided, following those discussions, that it did not wish to continue on this course. . . .

Recently, relations between the United Kingdom and Argentina deteriorated as a result of an incident in South Georgia, one of the Dependencies of the Falkland Islands, which is over 1,300 km from the Falkland Islands themselves. The United Kingdom has exercised sovereignty over South Georgia since 1775, when the island was discovered by Captain Cook. A British government station has existed on South Georgia since 1909. At present a British Antarctic Survey base provides an all-the-year-round British presence. The Argentine claim to South Georgia dates only from 1927 and is presumably based on the island's alleged proximity to the Argentine mainland.

The commander of the British Antarctic Survey base at Grytviken, on South

---

[1] *Established in 1961, the Committee of 24 advises the General Assembly on the implementation of its 1960 resolution (No 1514) on the granting of independence to colonial peoples.*

Georgia, reported on 19 March that an Argentine navy cargo vessel was anchored in nearby Leith Harbour and that a large party of Argentines were setting up camp. The Argentine flag had been hoisted. The base commander told the men they had no right to land on South Georgia without seeking permission from the British authorities and ordered them either to seek the necessary clearance or to leave. The United Kingdom Government sought immediate clarification from the Argentine Government, both in Buenos Aires and London, making clear that we regarded this as a potentially serious incident and asking the Argentines to arrange for the immediate departure of the ship and party. HMS *Endurance*, a lightly armed ice-patrol vessel, was ordered into the area.

The Argentine ship and most of the party left on 21 March. But about 10 Argentines remained. The Argentine Government, which claimed to have had no prior knowledge of the landing, assured us that no serving military personnel were involved: the men were working for a commercial company which has a contract to remove equipment from disused whaling stations on South Georgia. It was however unreasonable, the Argentine Government stated, to expect the Argentine Government to seek our authorisation for their presence on territory claimed by Argentina.

We made clear to the Argentine Government that we could not allow even the now small number of men to remain and told them that HMS *Endurance* was under way to the area and that the captain had been instructed that, if the Argentines failed themselves to arrange for the men's departure or regularise their position, he should as a last resort take the men on board, without using force, and return them to Argentina via Port Stanley, the capital of the Falkland Islands. The Argentine Government replied that they would regard this as gravely provocative. We assured them, in turn, that we wished, if at all possible, to prevent any escalation of this incident, but that the men had to be removed soon. If the Argentine Government could devise a method of doing so, we would be prepared to permit it. If not, the captain of HMS *Endurance* would have to carry out his instructions. I should like to emphasise at this point that HMS *Endurance* has played no active part in this incident. She has not approached the Argentine party at Leith but has been standing by well away from them.

On 25 March an Argentine naval transport vessel arrived at Leith Harbour to deliver further supplies to the men ashore. The British Ambassador in Buenos Aires sought an early response from the Argentine Government to our previous requests that they should arrange for the men's departure. This request was refused. The British Ambassador made it clear to the Argentine Government that we wished to do everything we could to avoid confrontation and proposed that if the party requested the proper authorisation from the British authorities at Grytviken, this would be given. No immediate reply was received from the Argentine Government.

But on 26 March the Argentine Government issued a press statement announcing that the Argentine party would be given all necessary protection by the Argentine Government. The Argentine press reported that Argentine naval vessels had been ordered into the area.

On 28 March the Argentine Foreign Minister sent a message to Lord Carrington, the British Foreign and Commonwealth Secretary, rejecting the British proposal to regularise the presence of the Argentine citizens in South Georgia but pressing instead for discussion not only of this issue but also of the wider sovereignty issue.

On 30 March statements in both Houses of Parliament in London made it clear that the British Government had no wish to interfere with a straightforward commercial contract but that we could not accept an illegal unauthorised presence on British territory. The statement emphasised our wish to defuse the issue and to pursue a diplomatic solution to it.

On 31 March the British Ambassador in Buenos Aires proposed to the Argentine Foreign Minister that a senior official should visit Buenos Aires to discuss a diplomatic solution, adding that the defusing of this incident would help prepare the way for resumption of a dialogue on the broader sovereignty issue.

Earlier today the Argentine Foreign Minister gave the reply of his Government to the British Ambassador in Buenos Aires. His reply was negative. He declined to discuss further the problems occasioned by the illegal presence of Argentine nationals on South Georgia. He specifically stated that he no longer wished to use diplomatic channels to discuss the situation in South Georgia.

I have described in some detail this recent incident affecting South Georgia. But the purpose of my Government in calling this meeting of the Security Council is to consider the threat not to South Georgia but to the Falkland Islands, which, as I have already said, are more than 1,300 km away. We have evidence that the Argentine Navy is about to launch an invasion, possibly as early as tomorrow morning. The Argentine press has for several days been carrying not only detailed accounts of Argentine naval movements 'in readiness for operations in the South Atlantic' but also statements by the Argentine Minister of Defence about the significance of these movements. On 28 March all naval leave was cancelled.

It is clear that almost all the Argentine fleet, including an aircraft carrier, destroyers, corvettes and submarines, is now at sea. Yesterday all Argentina's C130 transport aircraft left their bases. Their destination was not revealed but according to the Argentine press they are being prepared to airlift troops to the southern part of the country. On 30 March at least two aircraft of the Argentine air force overflew the Falkland Islands, without diplomatic clearance having been sought in accordance with normal international procedures. One of these overflights was by night and the aircraft carried no lights. All this activity, and the statements by Argentine ministers that have accompanied it, have given my Government reason to believe that an attempt is about to be made to use force to change the administration of the Falkland Islands against the wishes of the inhabitants.

My Government views the present situation with the utmost seriousness. We call on the Security Council to take immediate action in order to prevent an invasion. We ask this Council to exercise its responsibility under the Charter to maintain international peace and security. We ask this Council to call upon the Government of Argentina to refrain from the threat or use of force against the Falkland Islands and to exercise restraint. I can assure the Council that my Government has conducted the recent negotiations in perfect good faith and that the British Government stands ready to continue these negotiations in the future. What is unacceptable is an attempt to change the situation by force.

This morning the Secretary-General summoned the . . . distinguished representative of Argentina and myself separately to express his deep concern over the situation in the South Atlantic and to urge restraint on both sides. At noon today he issued a statement urging the two Governments to continue to use diplomatic means to resolve the outstanding issues between the two countries. I am authorised to inform [the Council] that it is the fervent wish of my Government to use diplomatic channels to resolve outstanding issues and to avert a crisis. As I have just described to the Council, my Government has made repeated efforts to engage the Argentine Government in the search for a diplomatic solution. These efforts have been rebuffed this morning in Buenos Aires.

It is this refusal of the Argentine Government to pursue the path of negotiation, combined with its disturbing naval and military preparations, which have led my Government to request this urgent meeting of the Security Council. We ask the Council to call upon the Government of Argentina to exercise the utmost restraint and to refrain from the use or threat of force in the South Atlantic. This is the way for the Council to give an appropriate response to this menacing situation in the area.

5. Statement of 1 April 1982 by the President of the Security Council, Mr Kamanda wa Kamanda, appealing to Argentina and Britain to continue the search for a diplomatic solution

After holding consultations with members of the Council, I have been authorised to make the following statement on behalf of the Council:

'The Security Council has heard statements from the representatives of the United Kingdom and Argentina about the tension which has recently arisen between the two Governments.

'The Security Council has taken note of the statement issued by the Secretary-General of the United Nations, which reads as follows:

"The Secretary-General, who has already seen the representatives of the United Kingdom and Argentina earlier today, renews his appeal for maximum restraint on both sides. He will, of course, return to Headquarters at any time, if the situation demands it."

'The Security Council, mindful of its primary responsibility under the Charter of the United Nations for the maintenance of international peace and security, expresses its concern about the tension in the region of the Falkland Islands (Islas Malvinas). The Security Council accordingly calls on the Governments of Argentina and the United Kingdom to exercise the utmost restraint at this time and in particular to refrain from the use or threat of force in the region and to continue the search for a diplomatic solution.

'The Security Council will remain seized of the question.'

6. Sir Anthony Parsons's response of 1 April 1982 to the appeal by the President of the Security Council

First I should like to reiterate what I said in my statement, namely that it is the fervent wish of my Government to use diplomatic channels to solve outstanding issues and to avert a crisis.

My Government welcomes the statement just made by you, Mr President, and I can assure you that we will be guided by its terms. We will exercise the utmost restraint; we will, in particular, refrain from the use or threat of force in the region and we will continue the search for a diplomatic solution.

We are not aggressors, as my Argentine colleague has again and again suggested we are. What possible or conceivable reason could we have for aggressive intent against Argentina? We threaten nobody. We have no interest in the area except to protect the interests of the inhabitants of the Falkland Islands and to respect their freely expressed wishes.

My Argentine colleague and I could debate endlessly the rights and wrongs of history, and I doubt whether we would agree. I would hope, however, that he would be prepared here and now, as I have done, to respond positively on behalf of his Government to the appeal of the Secretary-General and to respond positively, as I have done, to the call made by you, Mr President, on behalf of the whole Council for abstention from the use or threat of force in the region and continuance of the search for a diplomatic solution.

7. Statement to the Security Council on 2 April 1982 by Sir Anthony Parsons condemning the Argentine invasion and calling for an immediate Council response

I made clear to the Council yesterday that my Government did not lightly call for immediate sessions of the Security Council. Our worst apprehensions, those apprehensions which led to our calling the Council into session, have now been realised. The Argentine Government has ignored the two appeals of the Secretary-General and the appeal launched by you, Mr President, last night in the name of the whole Council for restraint and for the avoidance of the threat or the use of force. As we sit here, a massive Argentine invasion of the Falkland Islands is taking place.

I cannot find words strong enough to express my Government's condemnation of this wanton act of armed force. It is a blatant violation of the United Nations Charter and of international law. It is an attempt to impose by force a foreign and unwanted control over 1,900 peaceful agricultural people who have chosen in free and fair elections to maintain their links with Britain and the British way of life.

Last night my distinguished Argentine colleague repeatedly accused my country of aggression. It would be extremely interesting to learn what form of aggression the 1,900 peaceful farmers of the Falkland Islands and the lightly armed garrison of less than 100 British soldiers were plotting against the Republic of Argentina to justify what I dare say my Argentine colleague will present as an act of self-defence in accordance with Article 51 of the United Nations Charter. Put in these terms there could be no-one in this room or elsewhere who will not recognise the utterly nonsensical nature of the Argentine case as deployed in this Council last night.

The Council faces an emergency. It must act at once. I now propose to read out a draft resolution which I am having circulated to members of the Council and which in view of the extreme gravity of the situation I strongly hope will be adopted unanimously today. Members of the Council will observe that in the interests of a quick and peaceful healing of this undoubted breach of the peace I have, notwithstanding my own very deep feelings on the subject, confined the draft resolution to bare essentials at this critical juncture. I hope that the statement I have just made, brief as it has been, will leave no-one in any doubt as to the strength of my delegation's and my Government's views on what has happened. I now read the draft resolution. I quote:

'The Security Council, recalling the statement made by the President of the Security Council on 1 April 1982 calling on the Governments of Argentina and the United Kingdom to refrain from the use or threat of force in the region of the Falkland Islands:

'Deeply disturbed at the reports of an invasion on 2 April 1982 by armed forces of Argentina:

'Determining that there exists a breach of the peace in the region of the Falkland Islands:

1 Demands an immediate cessation of hostilities:

2 Demands an immediate withdrawal of all Argentine forces from the Falkland Islands:

3 Calls on the Governments of Argentina and the United Kingdom to seek a diplomatic solution to their differences and to respect fully the purposes and principles of the Charter of the United Nations.'

8. Speech by the Prime Minister, Mrs Margaret Thatcher, opening an emergency debate on the Falklands crisis in the House of Commons on 3 April 1982

... The House meets this Saturday to respond to a situation of great gravity. We are here because, for the first time for many years, British sovereign territory has been invaded by a foreign power. After several days of rising tension in our relations with Argentina, that country's armed forces attacked the Falkland Islands yesterday and established military control of the Islands.

Yesterday was a day of rumour and counter-rumour. Throughout the day we had no communication from the Government of the Falklands. Indeed, the last message that we received was at 21.55 hours on Thursday night, 1 April. Yesterday morning at 8.33 am we sent a telegram which was acknowledged. At 8.45 am all communications ceased. I shall refer to that again in a moment. By late afternoon yesterday it became clear that an Argentine invasion had taken place and that the lawful British Government of the Islands had been usurped.

I am sure that the whole House will join me in condemning totally this unprovoked aggression by the Government of Argentina against British territory. It has not a shred of justification and not a scrap of legality.

It was not until 8.30 this morning, our time, when I was able to speak to the Governor, who had arrived in Uruguay, that I learnt precisely what had happened. He told me that the Argentines had landed at approximately 6 am Falklands' time, 10 am our time. One party attacked the capital from the landward side and another from the seaward side. The Governor then sent a signal to us which we did not receive.

Communications had ceased at 8.45 am our time. It is common for atmospheric conditions to make communications with Port Stanley difficult. Indeed, we had been out of contact for a period the previous night.

The Governor reported that the Marines, in the defence of Government House, were superb. He said that they acted in the best traditions of the Royal Marines. They inflicted casualties, but those defending Government House suffered none. He had kept the local people informed of what was happening through a small local transmitter which he had in Government House. He is relieved that the Islanders heeded his advice to stay indoors. Fortunately, as far as he is aware, there were no civilian casualties. When he left the Falklands, he said that the people were in tears. They do not want to be Argentine. He said that the Islanders are still tremendously loyal. I must say that I have every confidence in the Governor and the action that he took.

I must tell the House that the Falkland Islands and their Dependencies remain British territory. No aggression and no invasion can alter that simple fact. It is the Government's objective to see that the Islands are freed from occupation and are returned to British administration at the earliest possible moment.

Argentina has, of course, long disputed British sovereignty over the Islands. We have absolutely no doubt about our sovereignty, which has been continuous since 1833. Nor have we any doubt about the unequivocal wishes of the Falkland Islanders, who are British in stock and tradition, and they wish to remain British in allegiance. We cannot allow the democratic rights of the Islanders to be denied by the territorial ambitions of Argentina.

Over the past 15 years, successive British Governments have held a series of meetings with the Argentine Government to discuss the dispute. In many of these meetings elected representatives of the Islanders have taken part. We have always made it clear that their wishes were paramount and that there would be no change in sovereignty without their consent and without the approval of the House.

The most recent meeting took place this year in New York at the end of February between my hon. Friend the Member for Shoreham (Mr Luce), accompanied by two members of the Islands council, and the Deputy Foreign Secretary of Argentina. The atmosphere at the meeting was cordial and positive, and a communiqué was issued about future negotiating procedures....

There was a good deal of bellicose comment in the Argentine press in late February and early March, about which my hon. Friend the Minister of State for Foreign and Commonwealth Affairs expressed his concern in the House on 3 March following the Anglo-Argentine talks in New York. However, this has not been an uncommon situation in Argentina over the years. It would have been absurd to dispatch the fleet every time there was bellicose talk in Buenos Aires. There was no good reason on 3 March to think that an invasion was being planned, especially against the background of the constructive talks on which my hon. Friend had just been engaged [see p 2]. ...

There had, of course, been previous incidents affecting sovereignty before the one in South Georgia, to which I shall refer in a moment. In December 1976 the Argentines illegally set up a scientific station on one of the Dependencies within the Falklands group —Southern Thule. The Labour Government attempted to solve the matter through diplomatic exchanges, but without success. The Argentines remained there and are still there.

Two weeks ago—on 19 March—the latest in this series of incidents affecting sovereignty occurred; and the deterioration in relations between the British and Argentinian Governments which culminated in yesterday's Argentinian invasion began. The incident appeared at the start to be relatively minor. But we now know it was the beginning of much more.

The commander of the British Antarctic Survey base at Grytviken on South Georgia —a dependency of the Falkland Islands over which the United Kingdom has exercised sovereignty since 1775 when the island was discovered by Captain Cook—reported to us that an Argentine navy cargo ship had landed about 60 Argentines at nearby Leith Harbour. They had set up camp and hoisted the Argentine flag. They were there to carry out a valid commercial contract to remove scrap metal from a former whaling station.

The leader of the commercial expedition, Davidoff, had told our Embassy in Buenos Aires that he would be going to South Georgia in March. He was reminded of the need to obtain permission from the immigration authorities on the island. He did not do so. The base commander told the Argentines that they had no right to land on South Georgia without the permission of the British authorities. They should go either to Grytviken to get the necessary clearances, or leave. The ship and some 50 of them left on 22 March. Although about 10 Argentines remained behind, this appeared to reduce the tension.

In the meantime, we had been in touch with the Argentine Government about the incident. They claimed to have had no prior knowledge of the landing and assured us that there were no Argentine military personnel in the party. For our part we made it clear that, while we had no wish to interfere in the operation of a normal commercial contract, we could not accept the illegal presence of these people on British territory.

We asked the Argentine Government either to arrange for the departure of the remaining men or to ensure that they obtained the necessary permission to be there. Because we recognised the potentially serious nature of the situation, HMS *Endurance* was ordered to the area. We told the Argentine Government that if they failed to regularise the position of the party on South Georgia or to arrange for their departure HMS *Endurance* would take them off, without using force, and return them to Argentina.

This was, however, to be a last resort. We were determined that this apparently minor problem of 10 people on South Georgia in pursuit of a commercial contract should not be allowed to escalate and we made it plain to the Argentine Government that we wanted to achieve a peaceful resolution of the problem by diplomatic means. To help in this, HMS *Endurance* was ordered not to approach the Argentine party at Leith but to go to Grytviken.

But it soon became clear that the Argentine Government had little interest in trying to solve the problem. On 25 March another Argentine navy ship arrived at Leith to deliver supplies to the 10 men ashore. Our Ambassador in Buenos Aires sought an early response from the Argentine Government to our previous requests that they should arrange for the men's departure. This request was refused. Last Sunday, on Sunday 28 March, the Argentine Foreign Minister sent a message to my right hon. and noble Friend the Foreign Secretary refusing outright to regularise the men's position. Instead it restated Argentina's claim to sovereignty over the Falkland Islands and their Dependencies.

My right hon. and noble Friend the Foreign and Commonwealth Secretary then sent a message to the United States Secretary of State asking him to intervene and to urge restraint.

By the beginning of this week it was clear that our efforts to solve the South Georgia dispute through the usual diplomatic channels were getting nowhere. Therefore, on Wednesday 31 March my right hon. and noble Friend the Foreign Secretary proposed to the Argentine Foreign Minister that we should dispatch a special emissary to Buenos Aires.

Later that day we received information which led us to believe that a large number of Argentine ships, including an aircraft carrier, destroyers, landing craft, troop carriers and submarines were heading for Port Stanley. I contacted President Reagan that evening and asked him to intervene with the Argentine President directly. We promised, in the meantime, to take no action to escalate the dispute for fear of precipitating the very event that our efforts were directed to avoid.

... On Thursday, the Argentine Foreign Minister rejected the idea of an emissary and told our Ambassador that the diplomatic channel, as a means of solving this dispute, was closed. President Reagan had a very long telephone conversation, of some 50 minutes, with the Argentine President, but his strong representations fell on deaf ears. I am grateful to him and to Secretary Haig for their strenuous and persistent efforts on our behalf.

On Thursday, the United Nations Secretary-General, Mr Pérez de Cuellar, summoned both British and Argentine permanent representatives to urge both countries to refrain from the use or threat of force in the South Atlantic. Later that evening we sought an emergency meeting of the Security Council. We accepted the appeal of its President for restraint. The Argentines said nothing. On Friday, as the House knows, the Argentines invaded the Falklands and I have given a precise account of everything we knew, or did not know, about that situation. There were also reports that yesterday the Argentines also attacked South Georgia, where HMS *Endurance* had left a detachment of 22 Royal Marines. Our information is that on 2 April an Argentine naval transport vessel informed the base commander at Grytviken that an important message would be passed to him after 11 o'clock today our time. It is assumed that this message will ask the base commander to surrender.

Before indicating some of the measures that the Government have taken in response to the Argentinian invasion, I should like to make three points. First, even if ships had been instructed to sail the day that the Argentines landed on South Georgia to clear the whaling station, the ships could not possibly have got to Port Stanley before the invasion....

Secondly, there have been several occasions in the past when an invasion has been threatened. The only way of being certain to prevent an invasion would have been to keep a very large fleet close to the Falklands, when we are some 8,000 miles away from base. No Government have ever been able to do that, and the cost would be enormous....

Thirdly, aircraft unable to land on the Falklands, because of the frequently changing weather, would have had little fuel left and, ironically, their only hope of landing safely would have been to divert to Argentina. Indeed, all of the air and most sea supplies for the Falklands come from Argentina, which is but 400 miles away compared with our 8,000 miles.

That is the background against which we have to make decisions and to consider what action we can best take. I cannot tell the House precisely what dispositions have been made—some ships are already at sea, others were put on immediate alert on Thursday evening.

The Government have now decided that a large task force will sail as soon as all preparations are complete. HMS *Invincible* will be in the lead and will leave port on Monday.

I stress that I cannot foretell what orders the task force will receive as it proceeds. That will depend on the situation at the time. Meanwhile, we hope that our continuing diplomatic efforts, helped by our many friends, will meet with success.

The Foreign Ministers of the European Community member states yesterday condemned the intervention and urged withdrawal. The NATO Council called on both sides to refrain from force and continue diplomacy....

We are now reviewing all aspects of the relationship between Argentina and the United Kingdom. The Argentine chargé d'affaires and his staff were yesterday instructed to leave within four days.

As an appropriate precautionary and, I hope, temporary measure, the Government have taken action to freeze Argentine financial assets held in this country. An order will be laid before Parliament today under the Emergency Laws (Re-enactments and Repeals) Act 1964 blocking the movement of gold, securities or funds held in the United Kingdom by the Argentine Government or Argentine residents.

As a further precautionary measure, the [*Export Credits Guarantee Department*] has suspended new export credit cover for the Argentine. It is the Government's earnest wish that a return to good sense and the normal rules of international behaviour on the part of the Argentine Government will obviate the necessity for action across the full range of economic relations....

29

The people of the Falkland Islands, like the people of the United Kingdom, are an island race. Their way of life is British; their allegiance is to the Crown. They are few in number, but they have the right to live in peace, to choose their own way of life and to determine their own allegiance. . . . It is the wish of the British people and the duty of Her Majesty's Government to do everything that we can to uphold that right. That will be our hope and our endeavour and, I believe, the resolve of every Member of the House.

9. Statement to the Security Council on 3 April 1982 by Sir Anthony Parsons urging the adoption of a resolution calling for an immediate cessation of hostilities, an immediate Argentine withdrawal and a resumption of the search for a diplomatic solution

... I would like to go back to the reason why I called for an immediate meeting of the Council two days ago. This was not, I repeat not, in any sense to discuss the rights or wrongs of the very long-standing issue between Britain and the Republic of Argentina over the Islands in the South Atlantic. This was not in any sense my intention.

I was summoned two or three days ago by the Secretary-General, acting on his own initiative and on a number of reports which had come to his notice. He extended to me a call to exercise restraint in what appeared to him to be an incipiently serious situation. Shortly after my conversation with the Secretary-General I received information through my Government that an armed attack by Argentina on the Falkland Islands was imminent. I therefore took what was an exceptional step for the British Government of asking the President of the Security Council for an immediate meeting. My only intention in seeking the meeting was that the Council should act in such a way as to pre-empt and deter any threat of the use of armed force and thus act in what is perhaps its finest role, to defuse dangerous situations. As has been said many times around this table, you issued an appeal on behalf of the whole Council the same evening, calling on both sides to exercise restraint and to refrain from the threat or use of force.

The following morning my delegation was disturbed to learn that this appeal had not been heeded by one party, and that Argentinian armed forces had invaded the Falkland Islands. My object in calling the Council a second time again had nothing whatsoever to do with the rights or wrongs of the long-standing issue between my country and the Republic of Argentina and was in no sense concerned with the merits of that issue. It was in response to this armed invasion. ...

I would like to go on to make one or two observations on certain points which the distinguished Foreign Minister of Argentina raised in his statement. I think I am right in saying that he suggested that the immediate origin of the present crisis was the incident which took place in South Georgia some days or even two or three weeks previously. I find that contention impossible to accept. This was an incident of relative triviality. It was a question of resolving what we, the United Kingdom Government, considered to be the illegal presence of 10 or 12 scrap metal dealers in the island of South Georgia. We had no intention of resolving this incident by the use of force. It would have been bizarre, indeed ludicrous, for the Government of the United Kingdom to bring an incident of that dimension to the Security Council. We had no doubt that we would be able to resolve it peacefully with the Government of the Republic of Argentina. And I cannot see how this very small dispute could conceivably justify the armed invasion of an inhabited group of islands, located some 800 miles away from the point at which the ten scrap metal dealers were located.

The distinguished Foreign Minister of Argentina also stated that his Government had not acted hastily in using force to assert their claim over the Falkland Islands. Earlier in his statement he referred to what he called our tactics of evasion and procrastination over the years. Of course, I cannot accept those charges and, at the risk of wearying the Council, I wish to give our side of the state of negotiations as they were before this very grave crisis exploded.

There was a meeting in New York at ministerial level between the British and Argentine Governments in late February this year, at which were present elected representatives of the people of the Falkland Islands. At the end of that meeting a joint communiqué [see p 17] was agreed between the two ministers who were conducting the negotiations. . . . The next thing that happened was that the Government of the Republic of Argentina unilaterally published [a] statement . . . [which] differed from the joint communiqué which we thought had been agreed at ministerial level in New York. It contained a final sentence, quoted by the distinguished Foreign Minister of Argentina, which read: 'However, should this not occur, Argentina reserves to terminate the working of this mechanism and to choose freely the procedure which best accords with her interests.' The fact that the Government of Argentina unilaterally published its own statement when we believed there would be a joint publication communiqué, and the presence in this statement of that final sentence, caused great alarm to the people of the Falkland Islands and indeed it caused apprehension within the British Parliament and apprehension in the British Government. We have since been trying to reconcile this issue and to get back to an agreed statement which would enable a negotiating process to begin. Unfortunately, we now find ourselves in the situation which we are today debating.

I would like to refer to another proposition which, if the interpretation was correct, I understood the distinguished Foreign Minister of Argentina to include in his statement. I understood him to say that the principles in the Charter (Article 2, paragraphs 3 and 4) were not necessarily applicable to situations which arose before the Charter was adopted. If my understanding is correct, I submit to members of the Council that this is an extremely dangerous doctrine. The world is at present beset by serious situations, some of which have from time to time developed into hostilities. In every continent in the globe, a large number of those situations have their origins years, decades, centuries before the United Nations Charter was adopted in 1945. If the use of force is to be valid for situations which originated before the Charter was adopted, I believe the world would be an even more dangerous and flammable place than it already is.

I said at the outset of my statement that I had not come here to enter into the rights and wrongs of the problem of sovereignty between the Republic of Argentina and my country. It has been very widely discussed by other speakers but I would like to say only one or two points which relate to it. The distinguished Foreign Minister of Argentina argued that the people of the Falkland Islands are not a population in international law. Those 18 or 19 hundred people are not recent arrivals in the Islands. The vast majority of them were born there, to families which have been there since the first half of the nineteenth century. In the judgment of my Government, whether they are 1,800 or 18,000 or 18,000,000, they are still entitled to the protection of international law and they are entitled to have their freely expressed wishes respected. These have been the only objectives of my Government in that area for a very long time. I cannot believe that the international community takes the view that Britain in the 1980s has a 'colonialist' or 'imperialist' ambition in the South Atlantic. The proposition is self-evidently ludicrous. We threaten nobody. We have merely concerned ourselves with the protection of the interest and respect for the wishes of the small population of the Islands.

Finally, it has also been argued that this was not an invasion because the Islands belong to Argentina. The fact is that the United Kingdom has been accepted by the

United Nations, by the General Assembly, by the Committee of 24 as the administering power. It flies in the face of facts to suggest that this was not an armed invasion.

The Council has before it a draft resolution, which I circulated to Council members yesterday. In response to a suggestion by the distinguished Foreign Minister of Panama, I have just asked the Secretariat to prepare a revised version of the text with the words 'Islas Malvinas' in parenthesis following the words 'Falkland Islands' wherever they occur, this being the standard United Nations practice in these matters.

Having said that I must affirm very strongly that my delegation wishes to have a vote on this draft resolution today. I do not want to sound self-congratulatory, but I think that my delegation has from the outset behaved with propriety. I responded to the first appeal of the Secretary-General. I responded to the appeal of the President. When I circulated the draft resolution yesterday my Government would have wished me to have a vote the same evening in the light of the gravity and urgency of the problem. When I was told that the distinguished Foreign Minister of Argentina was on his way here and wished to present his Government's case, and given that I had not given Council delegations the required 24 hours' notice, I agreed readily to postpone the vote until today.

So, I must ask very formally that, once the revised version of my text is circulated, we should hold an immediate vote on my resolution. We could thereafter consider the draft resolution presented by His Excellency the distinguished Foreign Minister of Panama. And if there were to be a general desire to vote on his resolution after the completion of the Council's business on mine, then I for one would be prepared to waive the 24 hours rule and vote on it today.

10.   Security Council Resolution 502 of 3 April 1982

The Security Council,

recalling the statement made by the President of the Security Council . . . on 1 April 1982 calling on the Governments of Argentina and the United Kingdom . . . to refrain from the use or threat of force in the region of the Falkland Islands (Islas Malvinas):

deeply disturbed at reports of an invasion on 2 April 1982 by armed forces of Argentina:

determining that there exists a breach of the peace in the region of the Falkland Islands (Islas Malvinas):

1   demands an immediate cessation of hostilities:

2   demands an immediate withdrawal of all Argentine forces from the Falkland Islands (Islas Malvinas):

3   calls on the Governments of Argentina and the United Kingdom to seek a diplomatic solution to their differences and to respect fully the purposes and principles of the Charter of the United Nations.

11. Speech by the Secretary of State for Foreign and Commonwealth Affairs, Mr Francis Pym, opening the House of Commons' second debate on the Falklands crisis on 7 April 1982

... The whole House and the country are struck by the appalling nature of the aggressive action the Argentine regime has committed. As recently as the end of February, as the House is aware, we had held talks with Argentina about the Falkland Islands. The Argentine Government were fully aware of Britain's position: that is to say, total firmness on the right of the Islanders to determine their own future; but, subject to that, willingness—indeed, desire—to deal with the Falkland Islands problem by means of fair negotiation.

Why did Argentina's ruler suddenly decide in the last days of March to resort to arbitrary and brutal aggression? I suggest that part of the answer lies in the very brutality and unpopularity of the Argentine regime itself. Inflation is raging in Argentina, at the rate of 140 per cent a year. The regime is notorious for its systematic contempt of all human rights. Since 1976, there have been thousands of arrests and killings, often described in a tragic and disgraceful euphemism as 'disappearances'. Only a few days before the invasion of the Falkland Islands there had been riots in Buenos Aires, and many people had been arrested. Harassed by political unrest at home, and beset by mounting economic difficulties, the regime turned desperately to a cynical attempt to arouse jingoism among its people. The Falkland Islanders have thus become the victims of the unprincipled opportunism of a morally bankrupt regime. Our purpose is to restore their rights.

Since the debate on Saturday, there have been a number of developments, and I should bring the House up to date. The Governor of the Falkland Islands and the Marines from Port Stanley have been evacuated to this country. I am sure that the whole House will wish to join me in paying tribute to them. ...

On Saturday, the Argentines occupied South Georgia. The small detachment of Royal Marines on that island put up a gallant and spirited resistance, but of course they could not stand up against overwhelming strength.

The Argentines have also been consolidating their presence in the Falkland Islands themselves. We believe that they may now have a sizeable occupation force. While we have no reports of direct maltreatment of the Islanders, it is quite obvious that the occupation force has no intention of treating them other than as a conquered population. Tight restrictions have been placed on their activities. It is essential, at the very least, that the Argentine authorities respect their international obligations to the civilian population.

The House is aware that we have dispatched a large task force towards the South Atlantic. We are confident that it will be fully adequate for any action that may be required in exercise of our undoubted right of self-defence under the United Nations Charter. While no formal state of war exists between this country and Argentina, we are fully entitled to take whatever measures may be necessary in the exercise of this right. This task force is an essential part of the means for attaining our objectives. It gives the strength from which to urge a settlement, and in the end it may only be strength that the regime in Argentina will understand.

There will be time before the task force reaches the area to do everything possible to solve the problem without further fighting. We would much prefer a peaceful settlement. We will do all we can to get one, and we shall welcome and support all serious efforts to that end. The House and the country should be in no doubt about that. But if our efforts fail, the Argentine regime will know what to expect: Britain does not appease dictators.

This is a tense and difficult period. We are using the interval immediately ahead for maximum diplomatic activity. The need is for all the world to bring pressure on Argentina to withdraw her armed forces from the Islands. Britain herself has already taken various measures. We have broken diplomatic relations with Argentina. The British Ambassador in Buenos Aires and most of his staff are being withdrawn. We have informed Argentina that its Consulates in Liverpool and Hong Kong must now be closed. I might add here that we have increased our broadcasts in Spanish to Argentina and in English to the Falkland Islands.

A small British interests section will continue to work in the Swiss Embassy, and we are most grateful to the Government of Switzerland, who are most expert in these matters, for agreeing to this arrangement. We have been advising the many British subjects living in Argentina to depart, unless they have special reasons for remaining. We have frozen all Argentine financial assets in this country. We have stopped new credit cover for exports to Argentina. We have banned the exports of arms to Argentina, and, as the House was informed yesterday, we have imposed an embargo on the import of all goods from Argentina from midnight last night.

The dispatch of our naval force and the economic measures we have taken should show the Argentine regime quite clearly that we mean business. Yet, if we are to convince it that aggression does not pay, we shall also need the support of the world community and all who believe in freedom.

The Security Council of the United Nations promptly and decisively endorsed the British view of the invasion of the Islands. It adopted—the very day after the invasion—a resolution put forward by Britain. That resolution demands an immediate cessation of hostilities and an immediate withdrawal of all Argentine forces, and it calls on the Governments of Argentina and the United Kingdom to seek a diplomatic solution to their differences and to respect the United Nations Charter. Britain immediately accepted the injunction to seek a diplomatic solution and observe the Charter.

But Argentina displayed her contempt for world opinion by coldly declaring that she would not comply with the resolution. The resolution is mandatory. It represents the expression of world opinion. It is binding in international law. I hope that the Argentine regime will be brought by the pressure of world opinion to fulfil its legal obligations.

The whole world has an interest in the fulfilment of this resolution. There are many such territories across the world which are vulnerable to aggression from more powerful neighbours. The preservation of peace depends on the exercise of responsibility and restraint. It depends on the strong not taking the law into their own hands and imposing their rule on the weak. It depends on the international community supporting the principle of self-determination and punishing those who wilfully and forcibly violate that principle. It is the Falkland Islanders who today are being deprived of their right to live in accordance with their wishes. If the world does not oblige Argentina to restore their rights, tomorrow it will be someone else's turn to suffer aggression and occupation. The world will become an even more dangerous place. . . .

Active discussion is now under way about measures by the European Community against Argentina. We have also been in close contact with the members of the Commonwealth, many of whom have responded with support, which bears witness to the strength and value of our Commonwealth links....

The case for other countries to follow Britain in taking economic measures is very strong. The Argentine economy depends greatly on export earnings and on raising finance to pay for imports and cover the external deficit. The scope for measures by our friends is extensive. About 40 per cent of Argentina's exports go to our major partners, including the members of the Community. Argentina frequently tries to raise funds in the leading financial centres of the Western world.

We are asking our friends to do everything they can to help us. They may not be able to take exactly the same measures as Britain herself. I do not think that precise similarity is necessarily the answer in this kind of situation, but the supply of arms and military equipment to Argentina must be stopped in present circumstances, and I hope that our friends and partners will encourage their banks to make no new loans to Argentina. I hope, too, that they will follow us in terminating official export credits. Above all, we are asking our friends and friendly countries to take measures against imports from Argentina. I ask also that they should announce what they are doing. This will impress Argentina, and encourage others to follow suit.

We are confident of the support of the world community and in particular of our friends. With this support, we hope to make it clear to Argentina that withdrawal from the Falkland Islands and a negotiated settlement constitute the only legal and acceptable approach in the dispute and the only one which is in Argentina's own interests.

The first responses to our approaches to friendly countries have been encouraging. Many countries across the world have condemned Argentina's aggression. Our friends in Europe and the United States were among the very first. New Zealand has severed diplomatic relations with Argentina. Canada has placed an immediate ban on military supplies. Canada and Australia have withdrawn their Ambassadors from Buenos Aires. The Netherlands, France, Belgium and [*the Federal Republic of*] Germany have taken action on arms sales. We hope that this list will soon grow much longer both in terms of action taken and the number of countries involved.

Meanwhile, our naval task force is on its way to the South Atlantic. It is a formidable demonstration of our strength and of our strength of will. The challenges which it may be called upon to face may also be formidable. I have no doubt that it will be equal to it. I know that the House will join me in offering full support to those who are now embarked in defence of British territory and to protect the rights which we and the Falkland Islanders hold equally dear.

It is intolerable that the peaceful people of the Falkland Islands, who are British by choice and by inheritance, should be the victims of unprovoked invasion by a powerful and covetous neighbour. It will be far from easy to reverse this situation. The difficulties speak for themselves. We shall spare no effort to reach a peaceful solution. The Falkland Islanders have reacted with courage and dignity to the rape of the Islands. I assure them now that Britain will stand by them. We have always said that their wishes are paramount. We shall do all in our power to show that their confidence in us is justified.

I know that our objective of liberating the Islands is shared in all parts of this House. If we in this country are to achieve our objective as swiftly and as peacefully as possible, then we must all unite in our resolve to succeed....

What we in Britain must now do, with the support and backing of all freedom-loving countries right across the world, is to see to it that Argentina's illegal and intolerable defiance of the international community and of the rule of law is not allowed to stand.

12. Maritime exclusion zone: Extract from speech by the Secretary of State for Defence, Mr John Nott, in the House of Commons on 7 April 1982

We are now deploying to the South Atlantic a powerful task group and other naval units capable of a range of operations. Should it become necessary, we shall use force to achieve our objective. We hope that it will not come to that. We hope that diplomacy will succeed. Nevertheless, the Argentines were the first to use force of arms in order to establish their present control of the Falklands. The Islands are now subject to an illegal and alien military rule. That is a position which must not endure for one day longer than is necessary.

Our first naval action will therefore be intended to deny the Argentine forces on the Falklands the means of reinforcement and re-supply from the mainland. To this end, I must tell the House that through appropriate channels the following notice is being promulgated to all shipping forthwith:

'From 0400 Greenwich Mean Time on Monday 12 April 1982, a maritime exclusion zone will be established around the Falkland Islands. The outer limit of this zone is a circle of 200 nautical mile radius from latitude 51 degrees 40 minutes South, 59 degrees 30 minutes West, which is approximately the centre of the Falkland Islands. From the time indicated, any Argentine warships and Argentine naval auxiliaries found within this zone will be treated as hostile and are liable to be attacked by British forces. This measure is without prejudice to the right of the United Kingdom to take whatever additional measures may be needed in exercise of its right of self-defence, under Article 51 of the United Nations Charter.'

13. Speech by Mrs Margaret Thatcher opening the House of Commons' third debate on the Falklands crisis on 14 April 1982

It is right, at this time of grave concern over the Falkland Islands and their people, that Parliament should be recalled so that the Government may report and the House may discuss the latest developments.

Our objective, endorsed by all sides of the House in recent debates, is that the people of the Falkland Islands shall be free to determine their own way of life and their own future. The wishes of the Islanders must be paramount. But they cannot be freely expressed, let alone implemented, while the present illegal Argentine occupation continues.

That is why our immediate goal in recent days has been to secure the withdrawal of all Argentine forces in accordance with resolution 502 of the United Nations Security Council and to secure the restoration of British administration. Our strategy has been based on a combination of diplomatic, military and economic pressures and I would like to deal with each of these in turn.

First of all, we seek a peaceful solution by diplomatic effort. This, too, is in accordance with the Security Council resolution. In this approach we have been helped by the widespread disapproval of the use of force which the Argentine aggression has aroused across the world, and also by the tireless efforts of Secretary of State Haig who has now paid two visits to this country and one to Buenos Aires.

On his first visit last Thursday we impressed upon him the great depth of feeling on this issue, not only of Parliament but of the British people as a whole. We may not express our views in the same way as the masses gathered in Buenos Aires, but we feel them every bit as strongly—indeed, even more profoundly, because Britons are involved. We made clear to Mr Haig that withdrawal of the invaders' troops must come first; that the sovereignty of the Islands is not affected by the act of invasion; and that when it comes to future negotiations what matters most is what the Falkland Islanders themselves wish.

On his second visit on Easter Monday and yesterday, Mr Haig put forward certain ideas as a basis for discussion—ideas concerning the withdrawal of troops and its supervision, and an interim period during which negotiations on the future of the Islands would be conducted. Our talks were long and detailed, as the House would expect. Some things we could not consider because they flouted our basic principles. Others we had to examine carefully and suggest alternatives. The talks were constructive and some progress was made. At the end of Monday, Mr Haig was prepared to return to Buenos Aires in pursuit of a peaceful solution.

Late that night, however, Argentina put forward to him other proposals which we could not possibly have accepted, but yesterday, the position appeared to have eased. Further ideas are now being considered and Secretary Haig has returned to Washington before proceeding, he hopes shortly, to Buenos Aires. That meeting, in our view, will be crucial.

These discussions are complex, changing and difficult, the more so because they are taking place between a military junta and a democratic government of a free people —one which is not prepared to compromise that democracy and that liberty which the British Falkland Islanders regard as their birthright.

We seek, and shall continue to seek, a diplomatic solution, and the House will realise that it would jeopardise that aim were I to give further details at this stage. Indeed, Secretary Haig has been scrupulous in his adherence to confidentiality in pursuit of the larger objective. We shall continue genuinely to negotiate through the good offices of Mr Haig, to whose skill and perseverance I pay warm tribute.

Diplomatic efforts are more likely to succeed if they are backed by military strength. At 5 am London time on Monday 12 April, the maritime exclusion zone of 200 miles around the Falkland Islands came into effect. From that time any Argentine warships and Argentine naval auxiliaries found within this zone are treated as hostile and are liable to be attacked by British forces.

We see this measure as the first step towards achieving the withdrawal of Argentine forces. It appears to have exerted influence on Argentina, whose navy has been concentrated outside the zone. If the zone is challenged, we shall take that as the clearest evidence that the search for a peaceful solution has been abandoned. We shall then take the necessary action. Let no-one doubt that.

The naval task force is proceeding with all speed towards the South Atlantic. It is a formidable force, comprising two aircraft carriers, five guided missile destroyers, seven frigates, an assault ship with five landing ships, together with supporting vessels. The composition of the force and the speed with which it was assembled and put to sea clearly demonstrate our determination. . . .

Our diplomacy is backed by strength, and we have the resolve to use that strength if necessary.

The third aspect of our pressure against Argentina has been economic. We have been urging our friends and allies to take action parallel to our own, and we have achieved a heartening degree of success. The most significant measure has been the decision of our nine partners in the European Community to join us not just in an arms embargo but also in stopping all imports from Argentina.

This is a very important step, unprecedented in its scope and the rapidity of the decision. Last year about a quarter of all Argentina's exports went to the European Community. The effect on Argentina's economy of this measure will therefore be considerable, and cannot be without influence on her leaders in the present crisis. I should like warmly to thank our European partners for rallying to our support. It was an effective demonstration of Community solidarity.

The decision cannot have been easy for our partners, given the commercial interests at stake, but they were the first to realise that if aggression were allowed to succeed in the Falkland Islands, it would be encouraged the world over.

Other friends too have been quick to help, and I should like to thank Australia, New Zealand and Canada for their sturdy and swift action. They have decided to ban imports from Argentina, to stop export credits and to halt all sales of military equipment. New Zealand has also banned exports to Argentina. We are grateful also to many other countries in the Commonwealth which have supported us by condemning the Argentine invasion.

What have the Argentines been able to produce to balance this solidarity in support of our cause? Some Latin American countries have, of course, repeated their support for the Argentine claim to sovereignty. We always knew they would. But only one of them has supported the Argentine invasion, and nearly all have made clear their distaste and disapproval that Argentina should have resorted to aggression.

Almost the only country whose position has been shifting towards Argentina is the

Soviet Union. We can only guess at the cynical calculations which lie behind this move. But Soviet support for Argentina is hardly likely to shake the world's confidence in the justice of our cause and it will not alter our determination to achieve our objectives. . . .

Recently the Government received a message from the British Community Council in Argentina urging a peaceful solution to the present conflict and asking that due consideration be given to the strong British presence in Argentina and the size of the British community there. We have replied, recognising the contribution which the British community has made to the development of Argentina—but making it plain that we have a duty to respond to the unprovoked aggression against the Falkland Islands and insisting that Argentina should comply with the mandatory resolution of the Security Council calling upon it to withdraw its troops. . . .

We are also being urged in some quarters to avoid armed confrontation at all costs, and to seek conciliation. Of course, we too want a peaceful solution, but it was not Britain who broke the peace. If the argument of no force at any price were to be adopted at this stage it would serve only to perpetuate the occupation of those very territories which have themselves been seized by force.

In any negotiations over the coming days we shall be guided by the following principles. We shall continue to insist on Argentine withdrawal from the Falkland Islands and Dependencies. We shall remain ready to exercise our right to resort to force in self-defence under Article 51 of the United Nations Charter until the occupying forces leave the Islands. Our naval task force sails on towards its destination. We remain fully confident of its ability to take whatever measures may be necessary. Meanwhile, its very existence and its progress towards the Falkland Islands reinforce the efforts we are making for a diplomatic solution.

That solution must safeguard the principle that the wishes of the Islanders shall remain paramount. There is no reason to believe that they would prefer any alternative to the resumption of the administration which they enjoyed before Argentina committed aggression. It may be that their recent experiences will have caused their views on the future to change, but until they have had the chance freely to express their views, the British Government will not assume that the Islanders' wishes are different from what they were before.

We have a long and proud history of recognising the right of others to determine their own destiny. Indeed, in that respect, we have an experience unrivalled by any other nation in the world. But that right must be upheld universally, and not least where it is challenged by those who are hardly conspicuous for their own devotion to democracy and liberty.

The eyes of the world are now focused on the Falkland Islands. Others are watching anxiously to see whether brute force or the rule of law will triumph. Wherever naked aggression occurs it must be overcome. The cost now, however high, must be set against the cost we would one day have to pay if this principle went by default. That is why, through diplomatic, economic and, if necessary, through military means, we shall persevere until freedom and democracy are restored to the people of the Falkland Islands.

14. The right of self-defence: Message of 23 April 1982 from the British Government to the Argentine Government[1]

In announcing the establishment of a maritime exclusion zone around the Falkland Islands, Her Majesty's Government made it clear that this measure was without prejudice to the right of the United Kingdom to take whatever additional measures may be needed in the exercise of its right of self-defence under Article 51 of the United Nations Charter. In this connection Her Majesty's Government now wishes to make clear that any approach on the part of Argentine warships, including submarines, naval auxiliaries or military aircraft which could amount to a threat to interfere with the mission of British forces in the South Atlantic will encounter the appropriate response. All Argentine aircraft, including civil aircraft engaging in surveillance of these British forces, will be regarded as hostile and are liable to be dealt with accordingly.

---

[1] *This document was immediately circulated in the Security Council and released publicly.*

15. Total exclusion zone: Statement by Mr John Nott in the House of Commons on 28 April 1982

The following statement was issued by the Government earlier today:

'From 1100 GMT on 30 April 1982, a total exclusion zone will be established around the Falkland Islands. The outer limit of this zone is the same as for the maritime exclusion zone established on Monday 12 April 1982, namely, a circle of 200 nautical miles radius from latitude 51 degrees 40 minutes South, 59 degrees 30 minutes West. From the time indicated, the exclusion zone will apply not only to Argentine warships and Argentine naval auxiliaries but also to any other ship, whether naval or merchant vessel, which is operating in support of the illegal occupation of the Falkland Islands by Argentine forces. The exclusion zone will also apply to any aircraft, whether military or civil, which is operating in support of the illegal occupation. Any ship and any aircraft whether military or civil which is found within this zone without due authority from the Ministry of Defence in London will be regarded as operating in support of the illegal occupation and will therefore be regarded as hostile and will be liable to be attacked by British forces.

'Also from the time indicated, Port Stanley airport will be closed; and any aircraft on the ground in the Falkland Islands will be regarded as present in support of the illegal occupation and accordingly is liable to attack.

'These measures are without prejudice to the right of the United Kingdom to take whatever additional measures may be needed in exercise of its right of self-defence, under Article 51 of the UN Charter.'[1]

---

[1] *On 7 May Britain announced that Argentine warships and aircraft found more than 12 nautical miles from the Argentine coast would be regarded as hostile (see p 12).*

16. Speech by Mrs Margaret Thatcher opening the House of Commons' fourth debate on the Falklands crisis on 29 April 1982

... During [*the last four weeks*] the Government have taken every possible step that had a reasonable prospect of helping us to achieve our objectives—the withdrawal of the Argentine forces and the end of their illegal occupation of the Islands, the restoration of British administration, and a long-term solution which is acceptable not only to the House but to the inhabitants of the Falkland Islands.

It is the Government's most earnest hope that we can achieve those objectives by a negotiated settlement. We have done everything that we can to encourage Mr Haig's attempts to find a solution by diplomatic means. ...

As the House knows, the Government have also taken military measures to strengthen our diplomatic efforts. Mr Haig's initiative would never have got under way if the British Government had not sent the naval task force to the South Atlantic within four days of Argentina's aggression against the Falkland Islands.

What incentive would there have been for the Argentine junta to give Mr Haig's ideas more than the most cursory glance if Britain had not under-pinned its search for a diplomatic settlement with the dispatch of the task force? Gentle persuasion will not make the Argentine Government give up what they have seized by force.

Our military response to the situation has been measured and controlled. On 12 April we declared a maritime exclusion zone. It has been enforced against Argentine warships and naval auxiliaries. It has been completely successful, and the Argentine forces on the Falkland Islands have been isolated by sea.

Eleven days later we warned the Argentine authorities that any approach by their warships or military aircraft which could amount to a threat to interfere with the mission of the British forces in the South Atlantic would encounter the appropriate response.

On 25 April . . . British forces recaptured South Georgia. The operation was conducted in exercise of our right of self-defence under Article 51 of the United Nations Charter. The minimum of force was used, consistent with achieving our objective, and no lives—Argentine or British—were lost in the operation . . .

The latest of our military measures is the imposition of the total exclusion zone round the Falkland Islands of which we gave 48 hours' notice yesterday. The new zone has the same geographical boundaries as the maritime exclusion zone which took effect on 12 April. It will apply from noon London time tomorrow to all ships and aircraft, whether military or civil, operating in support of the illegal occupation of the Falkland Islands. A complete blockade will be placed on all traffic supporting the occupation forces of Argentina. Maritime and aviation authorities have been informed of the imposition of the zone, in accordance with our international obligations.

We shall enforce the total exclusion zone as completely as we have done the maritime exclusion zone. The Argentine occupying forces will then be totally isolated —cut off by sea and air.

. . . On the diplomatic side, Mr Haig has put formal American proposals to the Argentine Government and requested an early response. I stress the status of those proposals. They are official American proposals. Mr Haig judged it right to ask Argentina to give its decision first, as the country to which Security Council resolution 502 is principally addressed. He saw Mr Costa Mendez last night, but no conclusion was reached. Mr Haig has also communicated to us the text of his proposals.

It is difficult both for the House and for the Government that we are not able to say more about them publicly, especially as in our democratic system we need the interplay of opinions and ideas. But they are Mr Haig's proposals, and we understand from him that it is his present intention to publish them in full. But he of course must judge the appropriate time.

The proposals are complex and difficult and inevitably bear all the hallmarks of compromise in both their substance and language. But they must be measured against the principles and objectives expressed so strongly in our debates in the House. My right hon. Friend the Secretary of State for Foreign and Commonwealth Affairs remains in close touch with Mr Haig. . . . It was the Argentine invasion which started this crisis, and it is Argentine withdrawal that must put an end to it.

The world community will not condone Argentina's invasion. To do so would be to encourage further aggression. As the Commonwealth Secretary-General said on 27 April—a point that was alluded to during Question Time today—

'In making a firm and unambiguous response to Argentine aggression, Britain is rendering a service to the international community as a whole.' . . .

As long as the Argentines refuse to comply with the Security Council resolution, we must continue to intensify the pressure on them. And we must not abandon our efforts to re-establish our authority over our own territory and to free our own people from the invader.

Let me turn now to the question of greater United Nations involvement. All our action has been based on a resolution of the United Nations. The Argentine invasion was carried out in defiance of an appeal issued by the President of the Security Council at our urgent request on 1 April. That solemn appeal was endorsed by the whole of the Security Council, but it was ignored. Immediately after the invasion we asked for another meeting of the Security Council. That meeting passed resolution 502. Since then our efforts and those of Mr Haig and a large part of the international community have been directed to implementing that mandatory resolution.

That resolution calls for Argentine withdrawal and a negotiated solution to the dispute. Without Argentine withdrawal, we have no choice but to exercise our unquestionable right to self-defence under Article 51 of the Charter. Of course, if Argentina withdrew we should immediately cease hostilities and be ready to hold negotiations with a view to solving the underlying dispute. After all, we were negotiating only a few weeks before the invasion.

It is quite wrong to suggest that because the invader is not prepared to implement the resolution the principles of the United Nations require that we, the aggrieved party, should forfeit the right of self-defence. Such an argument has no validity in international law. It would be to condone and encourage aggression and to abandon our people.

The question that we must answer is, what could further recourse to the United Nations achieve at the present stage ? We certainly need mediation, but we already have the most powerful and the most suitable mediator available, Mr Haig, backed by all the authority and all the influence of the United States, working to implement a mandatory resolution of the Security Council. If anyone can succeed in mediation, it is Mr Haig.

Of course, we support the United Nations and we believe that respect for the United Nations should form the basis of international conduct. But, alas, the United Nations does not have the power to enforce compliance with its resolutions, as a number of aggressors well know.

45

Those simple facts are perfectly well understood in the international community. Let me quote the Swedish Foreign Minister, because Sweden is a country second to none in its opposition to the use of force and its respect for the United Nations. The Swedish Foreign Minister said of the South Georgia operation:

'We have no objection to Britain retaking British territory. Time and again one is forced to observe that the United Nations is weak and lacks the authority required to mediate.'

That may not be desirable, but it is a fact of life and we must make our dispositions and judgments accordingly.

The recapture of South Georgia has not diminished international support. No country that was previously with us has turned against us. On Tuesday, my right hon. Friend [*Mr Pym*] was able to satisfy himself that the support of the European Community remained robust. The world has shown no inclination to condemn Britain's exercise of the right to self-defence.

In the Organisation of American States itself, Argentina was criticised for her use of force. Despite the claims of traditional Latin American solidarity, the only resolution passed clearly referred to Security Council resolution 502, and called on Argentina not to exacerbate the situation.

The truth is that we have been involved in constant activity at the United Nations. Our representative in New York has been in daily touch with the Secretary-General since the crisis began. He has discussed with him repeatedly and at length all possible ways in which the United Nations could play a constructive role in assisting Mr Haig's mission and, if Mr Haig fails, in securing implementation of resolution 502.

Sir Anthony Parsons has also discussed with Mr Pérez de Cuellar contingency planning about the part that the United Nations might be able to play in the longer term in negotiating and implementing a diplomatic settlement.

In the light of those discussions, our representative has advised us that, first, the Secretary-General is very conscious of the complexity of the problem and of the need for careful preparation of any initiative that he might take. Secondly, as the Security Council is already seized of the problem, it would be inappropriate for the Secretary-General to act under Article 99 of the Charter. Thirdly, the Secretary-General would not wish to take any initiative which he had not established in advance would be acceptable to both parties. Fourthly, the Secretary-General would also require a clear mandate from the Security Council before taking any action.

Our representative has also reported that the Secretary-General has several times stated in public that he was not prepared to take action while Mr Haig's mission was continuing.

. . . But if, at any time, either the Secretary-General or my right hon. Friend thought that a meeting between the two of them would be likely to assist in achieving an acceptable solution, then I say to the House that my right hon. Friend would of course go to New York straight away.

Although we have no doubt about our sovereignty over the Falkland Islands, South Georgia, South Sandwich or British Antarctic Territory, some of my right hon. and hon. Friends have suggested that we refer the matter to the International Court of Justice. Since Argentina does not accept the compulsory jurisdiction of the Court, the issue cannot be referred for a binding decision without her agreement.

We have never sought a ruling on the Falkland Islands themselves from that Court, but we have raised the question of the dependencies on three separate occasions—in 1947, 1949 and 1951. Each time Argentina refused to go to the Court.

In 1955, the British Government applied unilaterally to the International Court of Justice against encroachments on British sovereignty in the dependencies by Argentina. Again, the court advised that it could not pursue the matter since it could act only if there was agreement between the parties recognising the Court's jurisdiction.

In 1977, Argentina, having accepted the jurisdiction of an international court of arbitration on the Beagle Channel dispute with Chile, then refused to accept its results. It is difficult to believe in Argentina's good faith with that very recent example in mind.

There is no reason, given the history of this question, for Britain, which has sovereignty and is claiming nothing more, to make the first move. It is Argentina that is making a claim. If Argentina wanted to refer it to the International Court, we would consider the possibility very seriously. But in the light of past events it would be hard to have confidence that Argentina would respect a judgment that it did not like....

17. Speech by Mr Francis Pym closing the House of Commons' fourth debate on the Falklands crisis on 29 April 1982

This has been a thoughtful debate reflecting the gravity of the issues involved. . . .

There have been dissentient voices—rightly so—but the sense of the House has been supportive and in broad agreement. . . .

When I first spoke to the House as Foreign Secretary I said that I would approach my task over the Falkland Islands crisis in a spirit of determination and realism. The Government have tried to do that by applying all possible pressure with increasing intensity on the Argentine with the purpose of securing a negotiated settlement, if that is possible. We have applied and sustained a combination of pressures, all inter-related and growing in their effectiveness.

The first pressure that we applied immediately was diplomatic. Our first act after the invasion was to go to the United Nations, which has been an important element in the debate, where the Security Council responded to the aggression by passing resolution 502, which called, amongst other things, for immediate withdrawal from the Falkland Islands. That was a most important decision. Ever since, we and our friends around the world have lost no opportunity to press for its implementation and, wherever we can, to increase it.

The second type of pressure is economic. Our partners in the European Community and the Commonwealth—Australia, Canada and New Zealand—and also Norway joined us in banning imports from Argentina and taking other measures to show quite clearly that the whole world has an interest in reacting firmly to aggression. The pressure of those decisions is being maintained. The Assembly of the Council of Europe today passed, by an overwhelming majority, a resolution condemning Argentine aggression and expressing solidarity with Britain.

The third type of pressure is military. The task force that we assembled with record speed has advanced steadily towards the area of the Falklands. The scale of it and the competence with which it was assembled was the clearest demonstration of the professionalism of our forces . . . and the resolve of our nation. Ever since, we have continued to strengthen the force in various ways. The military pressure is still being stepped up. As has already been announced, a total exclusion zone will come into effect tomorrow.

I remind the House that the Government have made clear from the beginning that the pressure exercised on Argentina by our military preparations depended directly on our visible determination to be prepared to use force if we had to. Obviously, our whole intention is to obtain a peaceful settlement if we can, and the Argentine must be in no doubt about our resolution.

If Argentina had gained any impression that we were not so determined, any interest that she had in negotiations would evaporate. She cannot possibly have gained such an impression. We have steadily built up that military pressure by successive steps.

Meanwhile, we have exerted ourselves in every way that we can think of to achieve a peaceful settlement. The House is aware of the herculean efforts of Mr Haig to promote a negotiated settlement. He visited London twice and spent two periods in Buenos Aires. He has made and is continuing to make every possible attempt to bring about the implementation of resolution 502.

. . . My visit to Washington on 22 and 23 April was a part of that process. In my detailed discussions with Mr Haig, we covered all the elements that must be embodied in a settlement. We explored every possible angle, but the truth seems to be that although Britain and America have been working flat out for peace, Argentina has so far shown no indication of working seriously for a negotiated settlement. On the contrary, she has sustained a military build-up of reinforcements. In my view, that is a further and flagrant abuse of resolution 502. It is not just that Argentina has shown no sign of withdrawing, she has taken the positive step of increasing and increasing her military build-up. That is a flagrant abuse of the resolution.

Argentina's public statements show an unaltered insistence on intransigent positions and, above all, that the sovereignty of the Falklands belongs to her. Sovereignty does not belong to her. That is the heart of the dispute. The immediate position is that Argentina has not responded to the United States proposal that was put to her by Mr Haig on 27 April. While there is still some hope that Argentina might be willing to settle the crisis without the further use of force, I must tell the House that her current position is not encouraging.

I was greatly encouraged by the support that I encountered for Britain during my visit to the United States of America. The Americans are well aware that Argentina is the aggressor in this dispute and I imagine that they are greatly influenced by the ties of history and the shared ideals of freedom and democracy that link their country to ours. I have no doubt that those are some reasons why public opinion polls in America have shown such solid support for the United Kingdom. We are very grateful for it. . . .

After our re-taking of South Georgia by the carefully limited use of force—the minimum use of force is the present instruction and rules of engagement—Argentina surely abandoned any lingering doubts that Britain would exercise her right of self-defence. We shall certainly do so again if Argentina was so reckless as to violate the total exclusion zone. We are ready to do so if, unhappily, Argentina cannot be brought to accept a negotiated settlement. . . .

In the circumstances that I have described, it is not merely permissible for us to use our right of self-defence, it would be irresponsible for us not to exercise it and thus give a proper response to aggression. It is in the interests of the whole free world that the rule of law should be upheld and that aggression should not prevail. It is not just a British interest. The focus of attention is here because of the connection between Britain and the Falkland Islands, but it is an international interest. If we do not stand par excellence—which we do—for international law and order, and if other countries with the same interest in parliamentary democracy do not join us in this endeavour, the outlook for the world is bleak. It is precisely for that reason that our friends all round the world have supported us and why we expect that they shall continue to do so.

. . . The Secretary-General [*in a press statement issued on 26 April*] is absolutely right to call for the implementation of resolution 502. No one wants to achieve that more than we do. It is indeed central to all our efforts in the crisis . . . But there cannot be any suggestion that Britain and Argentina are on the same footing—the victim and the aggressor—that cannot be right.

It is not we who have refused to implement resolution 502—quite obviously it is the Argentines. So long as Argentina refuses to withdraw and holds on to the Islands, it is quite wrong for anyone to suggest that we should tie our hands and forgo in any way our inherent right of self-defence. . . .

Only the fact that we have maintained our right of self-defence unimpaired has brought the Argentine to consider the American proposals at all. If we gave up that right, who could believe that negotiations could continue for a moment longer? How could that possibly advance the cause of peace or strengthen the authority of the United Nations? I do not see how it could.

The Leader of the Opposition [*Mr Michael Foot*] asked whether we had fulfilled our obligation under Article 51 of the Charter to report to the Security Council the measures that we have taken in self-defence. . . . We have done so scrupulously. Our Permanent Representative in New York has successively notified the President of the Security Council of our proclaiming of the maritime exclusion zone, of our recovery of South Georgia and, most recently, of our announcement of a total exclusion zone to come into force tomorrow. . . .

The Leader of the Opposition also suggested that we should have gone to the United Nations to get the Security Council to impose economic sanctions on Argentina as a means of enforcing Argentine compliance with resolution 502. I can assure him that we have considered that possibility. But we saw at once that the Soviet Union, in its search for ways of strengthening its influence in Argentina, would certainly veto any such resolution. We have it in mind that that shadow is over the events in the South Atlantic. That would have meant that we would not have succeeded in our aim of increasing pressure on Argentina to fulfil its legal obligations. What we would have done would be to provide the occasion for a tightening of links between the Soviet Union and Argentina, which is not only not in our interests or Argentina's but is not, I think, in anyone else's interests.

The Leader of the Opposition . . . also advanced several ideas for involving the United Nations in a settlement of the Falkland Islands question. I have spent much time thinking about the various ways in which that might be done and the advantages and disadvantages of it. My right hon. Friend the Prime Minister has already covered in her opening speech the idea of recourse to the International Court of Justice [*see p 46*]. . . .

There is also the idea of a United Nations role in the administration of the Islands and the possibility of a United Nations trusteeship. . . . These options we have also considered, but they are, I think, for the longer term. Trusteeship is a complex business and takes a considerable time to work out. It has far-reaching implications. We for our part would be entirely prepared to look carefully at any ideas that would secure compliance with resolution 502 without doing violence to the principles that have been supported in this House. So far, however, we have had no indication that the idea of trusteeship would do the trick or have any acceptance whatever by the Argentines. So that that does not look very hopeful.

In short, we have considered a whole range of possible diplomatic options. We have always come back to the conclusion that it is Mr Haig who has the best opportunity. . . .

The House has had the chance on several occasions to consider in these debates the essential principles on which the Government should approach the complex problem of settling the Falkland Islands difficulty. The ideas which we discussed with Mr Haig and the proposals which he has put to the Government of Argentina have been measured against these principles. I am sure that the House is aware of the main elements which have evolved during these long talks. They are the arrangements for withdrawal, the arrangements for an interim administration and the arrangements under which the future status of the Islands might be discussed and negotiations for a long-term settlement continued and perhaps hopefully concluded. . . .

It goes without saying that there must be an immediate withdrawal of all Argentine forces as required by the basic resolution. Of course, the necessary time for that must be allowed. We for our part would be prepared to move British forces in parallel. At the same time, we have to ensure that there can be no change of heart or mind on the part of the Argentines during the process of withdrawal and, equally important, I suggest, that there should be no attempt or possibility of an attempt at reoccupation of the Islands at some future date. We have the immediate problem of the withdrawal of forces now, but we also have to think beyond that to the circumstances that might subsequently arise.

On the interim arrangements, the British administration was illegally displaced from the Islands by the Argentine invasion and must be restored. Withdrawal is the first priority and the British Government have to consider the practical arrangements that will follow after that withdrawal. It is not an easy matter. It is quite complicated, and much time in the discussions that have been going on in the last few weeks has been devoted to it. Provided that the principle of British administration is preserved, the Government are prepared to consider reasonable suggestions and ideas in this field. Indeed, I have been exploring them thoroughly with Mr Haig. . . .

The third area is the discussion about the status of the Islands in the future nego-tiations. Many hon. Members today and previously have rightly emphasised the principle of self-determination. Not only the Government and the House but also Congress and the people of the United States attach the highest importance to it. Our basic position is that Britain is ready to co-operate in any solution which the people of the Falkland Islands could accept and any framework of negotiation which does not predetermine and does not prejudice the eventual outcome. The prejudicing of that outcome is one of the sticking points of the Argentines which we cannot accept.

As my right hon. Friend the Prime Minister said, it is extremely discouraging that the latest statements from the Foreign Minister of Argentina lay even more stress than before on Argentine determination not to yield an inch on the question of sovereignty. It seems that he does not depart one iota from the position that there must be prior agreement that any negotiation must end in sovereignty being transferred to Argentina, regardless of the views of the people of the Falkland Islands on this point. The Argentines know, of course, and Mr Haig knows and has accepted, that this is a completely unacceptable position for us. That is perhaps the most fundamental issue of all that we face.

I should like to say a word or two about the Islanders . . . They are the ones who are under the jackboot of the invader. They have now been subjected to new restrictions, which is perhaps not altogether surprising, including a curfew and a blackout. I imagine that they are living a pretty miserable life.

It is our present understanding that the majority of the Islanders prefer to stay where they are, which is a remarkable testimony to their attachment to their Island. I cannot pretend that the total exclusion zone which comes into effect tomorrow has no implications for their well-being. Clearly it has. But I have every confidence that they will see why we have acted as we have, because it is for the sake of our common purpose and their main interest—to get the invader out.

It is our hope in the meantime that the International Red Cross will be able to establish a presence on the Islands, and that with its help, or by other means, we shall be able to arrange for the evacuation of any Islanders who may still wish to depart. 51

Transit through the total exclusion zone is possible with our permission. We shall control it, and if someone wanted to leave for any reason whatsoever with International Red Cross assistance we would do our best to make that possible. . . .

Many hon. Members have asked what the Government will do if Argentina rejects Mr Haig's proposals. Let me emphasise in reply that I very much hope that Argentina will take a reasonable view of her own interests and will not reject a negotiated settlement of the present crisis. If she did reject it, we would consider very carefully how to try to continue the negotiating process, but we have always made it clear that our objective is a settlement and the implementation of the mandatory United Nations resolution, and not the avoidance of hostilities at any price. If Argentina will not accept a negotiated solution, then reluctantly and with the greatest possible restraint, we must use force. But we shall not relax for a moment in our efforts for a peaceful solution. It is encouraging that today the House has supported us so staunchly in all our views.

18. Negotiations for a peaceful settlement: Statement by Mr Francis Pym in the House of Commons on 7 May 1982

The House is aware that, while we have mobilised and dispatched the task force to the South Atlantic, where it has already been involved in active operations, we have also been pursuing a highly active programme of consultation and negotiation in the search for a diplomatic solution to the present crisis.

The House has shown exemplary patience with my inability to explain the nature of the proposals that we have been examining. I now have to report to the House that Argentine intransigence has again led it to reject proposals for a diplomatic solution. In these circumstances, I think it is right that I should give the House an account of where we stand—and of where we intend to go from here.

The fact that we were able to reach a point where a new set of firm proposals could be put to both sides owes much to the tireless efforts of Mr Haig. We are also grateful for the constructive contributions of President Belaúnde of Peru. We also put forward practical ideas ourselves which take account of the Argentine position as well as our own.

Yesterday we signified that we were willing to accept and implement immediately an interim agreement which would prepare the way for a definitive settlement. Such an agreement would have demonstrated substantial flexibility on our part. If it had been accepted by the Argentines, the ceasefire, which would have been firmly linked to the beginning of Argentine withdrawal, could have come into effect as early as 5 o'clock this afternoon.

The interim agreement under discussion yesterday included the following elements: first, complete and supervised withdrawal of Argentine forces from the Falkland Islands, matched by corresponding withdrawal of British forces; secondly, an immediate ceasefire as soon as Argentina accepted the agreement and agreed to withdraw; thirdly, appointment of a small group of countries acceptable to both sides which would supervise withdrawal, undertake the interim administration in consultation with the Islander's elected representatives, and perhaps help in negotiations for a definitive agreement on the status of the Islands, without prejudice to our principles or to the wishes of the Islanders; fourthly, suspension of the existing exclusion zones and the lifting of economic sanctions.

This agreement would not, of course, have prejudged in any way the outcome of the negotiations about the future. As the House knows, that is a sticking point for us. Pending the outcome of the negotiations, the two sides would simply have acknowledged the difference that exists between them over the status of the Islands.

We have worked, and will continue to work, positively and constructively for a peaceful solution. Our agreement to these ideas makes this once again abundantly clear.

I wish I could say that the Argentine junta had been working in a similar spirit; clearly it was not. The Argentines have so far insisted that a transfer of sovereignty to them should be a precondition of negotiations on a final settlement. The Argentines talk much of the need for decolonisation of the Islands. What they appear to mean by this is colonisation by themselves.

In addition to this, the Argentines seem now to be obstructing progress in another but equally fundamental way. They appear to be asking for a ceasefire without any clear link with a withdrawal of their invasion force. To grant this would be to leave them indefinitely in control of people and territory which they had illegally seized, and to deny ourselves the right of pursuing our own self-defence under Article 51 of the Charter.

We have not allowed Argentine military activities to halt the measures which our task force is taking. We will not allow their diplomatic obstructionism to do so either. Nor will they be allowed to halt our vigorous endeavours to find a peaceful way out of the conflict into which they have led us. This is why I welcomed and co-operated wholeheartedly with the initiatives of Mr Haig, and why I now welcome the efforts of the Secretary-General of the United Nations and am working closely with him.

As the House knows, the Secretary-General has put to both us and Argentina some ideas as a framework around which progress might be made. The Argentine Government claim to have accepted these ideas. We are bound to be sceptical of this claim. There is no indication that Argentina has accepted either that she must withdraw, as resolution 502 demands, or that negotiations cannot, as Argentina insists, be made conditional on the transfer of sovereignty to her. Indeed, it is difficult to believe that Argentina, having rejected ideas devised by Mr Haig and the President of Peru, can now accept the Secretary-General's ideas which have such a similar basis.

For our part, we have accepted the general approach set out by the Secretary-General. I sent him yesterday a positive and substantive reply, making clear that the elements for a solution put forward by him were close to those which had been the basis of our efforts since the beginning of the crisis.

I made clear at the same time that in our view resolution 502 must be implemented without delay; that an unconditional ceasefire could not under any circumstances be regarded by us as a step towards this; and that implementation of a ceasefire must be unambiguously linked to the commencement of Argentine withdrawal which must be completed within a fixed number of days. I then went on to give details, which it would not be right to reveal to the House now, of what we would be prepared to accept to fill out the framework suggested by him.

If one phase of diplomatic effort has been brought to an end by Argentine intransigence, another phase is already under way in New York. The aim remains the same: to secure the early implementation of resolution 502. We are working urgently and constructively with the Secretary-General to this end. I hope the Argentines will henceforth show that readiness and desire to reach a peaceful settlement which so far has been evident only on our side. If they do not, then let them be in no doubt that we shall do whatever may be necessary to end their unlawful occupation. Our resolve is undiminished.

It remains the Government's highest priority to achieve an early negotiated settlement if that is humanly possible.

19. Speech by Mr Francis Pym opening the House of Commons' fifth debate on the Falklands crisis on 13 May 1982

. . . The Government have throughout the crisis taken every opportunity to keep the House informed of developments; and, although on this occasion there is not very much new that I can report, I welcome this further opportunity for debate on the very important issues that are involved. I say that despite the fact that the negotiations now in progress in New York are in an important and delicate phase.

I would also like to put on record the Government's gratitude, and my personal thanks, both for the support and co-operation that we have received from the House and for the resolute support that the British people have given us. This has been vital to the maintenance of our resolute stand.

The Government's position has remained clear and consistent throughout. Our objectives and our strategy are unchanging. We have of course adapted our tactics in the light of the evolving diplomatic and military circumstances. As the House knows, we have moved through different stages of negotiations: the first with Mr Haig in London and in Washington; then in reacting to the ideas first launched by the President of Peru and subsequently developed in discussion by him with the United States; and now the talks with the Secretary-General of the United Nations. Through all those stages and throughout this procedure we have shown a careful balance of firmness on the essential principles, tempered by the necessary measure of readiness to negotiate on issues where negotiation is possible. However, in all this negotiation our determination has never wavered—our determination and resolve to end Argentina's illegal occupation and to uphold the rights of the Falkland Islanders. . . .

From the beginning of this crisis, the Government have been trying, as the House well knows, to build up the pressures on Argentina steadily, progressively and remorselessly. Our aim has been to make it withdraw, through a negotiated arrangement if that can be achieved. The pressures we have applied have been of three kinds—diplomatic, economic and military.

The diplomatic pressures bring to bear the moral weight of world opinion upon Argentina and its act of aggression. Just as Security Council resolution 502 was clear and firm in its condemnation of aggression and its demands for Argentine withdrawal, so have the statements of our friends and allies in the ensuing weeks continued to demonstrate the world's expectation that Argentina will end its occupation of the Islands.

Last weekend I had full talks in private with the foreign ministers of the [*European Community*]. I was once again heartened by the expressions of solidarity and support I received. Europe remains on our side. Further evidence of that was provided by the European Parliament yesterday. It passed a resolution recognising that the loss of life in the South Atlantic—which we all regret—is due to the failure of the Argentines to comply with resolution 502. It also reaffirmed its previous tough resolution in our support and called on the foreign ministers to renew the import embargo on 17 May.

We have found no inclination among the leaders of the free world to blur the distinction between legitimacy and illegality, between self-defence and aggression, between right and wrong, and between truth and falsehood. The world knows that the international rule of law would be dangerously undermined if Argentine aggression were allowed to stand, and that it is on that international rule of law and its upholding, that the prospects for stability and prosperity for people depend.

International support for us remains firm. We continue to receive messages of support from Governments all around the world. The Commonwealth remains steadfast and resolute in its backing of our stand. . . .

The diplomatic pressure remains strong and sustained. So also does the economic pressure. . . . The suspension of imports, the denial of credit, the bans on arms sales—all those continue to have a real and biting effect on an Argentine economy already in disarray.

It was estimated earlier this year that Argentina would need to raise some $3,000 million in net new loans in 1982. World repugnance at its recent actions has meant that —so far as we can tell—not a single new public sector loan has been agreed since 2 April.

The Argentine peso has been under heavy pressure. Besides expectations of increased inflation and general loss of confidence, the markets of the world have indicated clearly what they think of the Argentine currency: while the official rate remains at 14,000 pesos to the American dollar, even across the River Plate in Montevideo the free market is demanding 20,000 pesos for the dollar.

Those who have given us economic support should not doubt that the consequence of this support has been extremely valuable in concentrating pressure on Argentina to comply with resolution 502. It is, in fact, an essential part of the pressure that we are applying in order to achieve an early negotiated solution.

The third element of our strategy is military. As the House knows we continue to tighten the military screw. British servicemen are experiencing danger and hardship 8,000 miles away. Their presence and their activity are making it increasingly hard and costly for Argentina to sustain its occupation of the Falkland Islands.

We all grieve over British losses. We take no satisfaction at the losses inflicted on Argentina. We regret them, too. As the net closes round the Islands military incidents may occur with increasing frequency. That may be inevitable in the circumstances. But we must never forget who is the aggressor, who invaded whom, who embarked on an unlawful and dangerous course, who first took up arms and thus put lives at risk, who fired the first shot. Argentina knows how to avoid further military conflict. It can begin its withdrawal—now.

The whole House and the country know our clear and decisive preference for a negotiated settlement. However, military pressure is necessary to bring Argentina to negotiate seriously and at the same time to strengthen our negotiating hand. I do not doubt that it is having this effect. There are signs that the message is beginning to get through.

We have been and remain indefatigable in the search for that negotiated settlement. I shall not recall now the long and strenuous efforts that we made in co-operation with Mr Haig, ending in failure because of Argentina's intransigence.

But it is interesting that, in spite of Argentina's rejection then, the elements of an agreement about which I first spoke to the House as long ago as 21 April have remained as elements in subsequent negotiations . . . the arrangements for an Argentine withdrawal, the nature of any interim administration of the Islands and the framework for negotiations on a long-term solution [see also pp 49–51 and 53–4]. . . .

The negotiations are now going on under the auspices of the Secretary-General of the United Nations. Señor Pérez de Cuellar has shown great determination and diplomatic ability in his lengthy and frequent talks in recent days with the British representative, Sir Anthony Parsons. They have met at least once every day and sometimes more often.

On Tuesday, those talks seemed to make a little progress. Yesterday, things went less well. Hopes have been raised before, only to be dashed, and many very serious difficulties remain. It would be quite wrong for me not to indicate that to the House....

I hope that more progress will be made—and quickly. If it is not, it will not be for lack of effort and readiness on our part to reach a negotiated solution. Nor have our efforts to this end in any way prejudiced or hindered the necessary build-up of military pressure. I want to assure the House that they have not closed off any military option, or affected our military options in any way.

It is not, of course, easy to negotiate with the Argentine authorities. While their representative in New York has appeared to be prepared to recognise many of the realities of the situation, there have been—even within the last two days—a number of unhelpful statements by other Argentine public figures, made in public.

On different occasions the Foreign Minister, one of his senior officials, a general and a junior minister in another department have all referred to the process of negotiation as if this was designed solely to lead up to a handover of sovereignty to Argentina. That attitude is, I repeat, quite unacceptable to us and we must be absolutely sure that Argentina does not adhere to it, privately or publicly, if a negotiated settlement is to be possible....

It would perhaps be helpful if once again I emphasise those basic requirements in our strategy which must be understood by Argentines as they have been understood by all reasonable people across the world. If Argentina now recognises that there are issues on which we remain wholly justifiably immovable, we may be able to make greater progress in other areas where some flexibility is possible.

The first absolutely fundamental requirement is the need for the withdrawal of the whole Argentine invasion force and civil personnel. We insist on this and until Argentina is committed to such a withdrawal, and is willing to commence it, we cannot commit ourselves to a ceasefire. When it demonstrates that that readiness to withdraw is a reality, we shall feel able and willing to match this—in ways yet to be determined—by standing our own forces off from the area of conflict.

The timings and the distances of mutual withdrawal are things which need to be settled and on which we are keen to make progress in negotiation. And the House will understand that we must be absolutely certain about arrangements for verification. After all, after the invasion, we cannot be expected to have faith in Argentine good intentions.

The second fundamental requirement, on which we are absolutely firm, is that the outcome of long-term negotiations about the future of the Islands must not be pre-judged in advance in any way....

That is a reasonable position and one on which we shall not compromise. It has been a fundamental issue throughout all the negotiations and a major problem in the negotiations. From the outset we have made our position entirely and unmistakably clear. Nevertheless, even at this point in time it is necessary for me to repeat it, because it is our immutable objective....

Argentine withdrawal from the Falkland Islands, once agreed, should be carried out within a fixed number of days. Negotiations about the long-term future of the Islands will, of necessity, take a matter of months. It follows from this—as I said in this House many days ago, on 21 April, and again in more detail on 7 May—that some interim arrangements will be necessary on the Islands. . . . I have already made clear on two previous occasions that we do not debar involvement of third parties in these arrangements. It may or may not be the case that the United Nations will have a role to play. But we could not, of course, agree to a structure, however temporary, which ignored the past and disregarded the administrative experience of the British inhabitants of the Islands. They know how to run their affairs in a democratic way. . . .

There are officials and administrators who know their jobs; there are democratically elected members of the councils who know the feelings of their fellow Islanders. They must be fitted in to whatever is agreed if the Islands are to be run fairly and efficiently during whatever interim period proves necessary. . . .

If we get an agreement, long-term negotiations may begin quite soon. I want to make clear to the House that we have no doubt whatever about the British title to sovereignty. All British Governments have taken the same view. However, we did not, before the invasion, rule out discussion of sovereignty in negotiations with Argentina. Again, successive governments of both parties have taken the same position. We still remain willing to discuss it as one of the factors in negotiations about the long-term future. . . .

Present negotiations in New York are at an important point. Our resolve has not wavered. There have been some indications—actually the first since the crisis began— of genuine Argentine willingness to negotiate on some of the important points. There will have to be more if we are to succeed.

The Government remain determined to see the implementation of the mandatory resolution of the Security Council. As before, we infinitely prefer to achieve this by negotiation, and we are bending our most strenuous efforts to this end. At the same time our military presence in the South Atlantic continues to become stronger.

. . . If, in the end, Argentine intransigence prevents success in negotiation, Argentina will know that the alternative is another kind of ending to the crisis. We do not want that, but we are ready for it. As it has been throughout this crisis, the choice lies with those who rule Argentina.

20. Falkland Islands: Proposed Interim Agreement. Draft agreement presented by the British Government to the United Nations Secretary-General on 17 May 1982[1]

The Government of the Republic of Argentina and the Government of the United Kingdom of Great Britain and Northern Ireland,

Responding to Security Council Resolution 502 (1982) adopted on 3 April 1982 under Article 40 of the Charter of the United Nations,

Having entered into negotiations through the good offices of the Secretary-General of the United Nations for an Interim Agreement concerning the Falkland Islands (Islas Malvinas), hereinafter referred to as 'the Islands',

Having in mind the obligations with regard to non-self-governing territories set out in Article 73 of the Charter of the United Nations...

Have agreed on the following:

Article 1

(1) No provision of this Interim Agreement shall in any way prejudice the rights, claims and positions of either Party in the ultimate peaceful settlement of their dispute over the Islands.

(2) No acts or activities taking place whilst this Interim Agreement is in force shall constitute a basis for asserting, supporting or denying a claim to territorial sovereignty over the Islands or create any rights of sovereignty over them.

Article 2

(1) With effect from a specified time, 24 hours after signature of this Agreement (hereinafter referred to as Time 'T'), each Party undertakes to cease and thereafter to refrain from all firing and other hostile actions.

(2) Argentina undertakes:

  (a) to commence withdrawal of its armed forces from the Islands with effect from Time 'T';

  (b) to withdraw half of its armed forces to at least 150 nautical miles away from any point in the Islands by Time 'T' plus 7 days; and

  (c) to complete its withdrawal to at least 150 nautical miles away by Time 'T' plus 14 days.

(3) The United Kingdom undertakes:

  (a) to commence withdrawal of its armed forces from the Islands with effect from Time 'T';

  (b) to withdraw half of its armed forces to at least 150 nautical miles away from any point in the Islands by Time 'T' plus 7 days; and

  (c) to complete its withdrawal to at least 150 nautical miles away by Time 'T' plus 14 days.

---

[1] *Published as Annex A of Document No 21 (see p 62).*

Article 3
With effect from Time 'T', each Party undertakes to lift the exclusion zones, warnings and similar measures which have been imposed.

Article 4
On the completion of the steps for withdrawal specified in Article 2, each Party undertakes to refrain from reintroducing any armed forces into the Islands or within 150 nautical miles thereof.

Article 5
Each Party undertakes to lift with effect from Time 'T' the economic measures it has taken against the other and to seek the lifting of similar measures taken by third parties.

Article 6
(1)   Immediately after the signature of the present Agreement, Argentina and the United Kingdom shall jointly sponsor a draft Resolution in the United Nations under the terms of which the Security Council would take note of the present Agreement, acknowledge the role conferred upon the Secretary-General of the United Nations therein, and authorise him to carry out the tasks entrusted to him therein.

(2)   Immediately after the adoption of the Resolution referred to in paragraph (1) of this Article, a United Nations Administrator, being a person acceptable to Argentina and the United Kingdom, shall be appointed by the Secretary-General and will be the officer administering the government of the Islands.

(3)   The United Nations Administrator shall have the authority under the direction of the Secretary-General to ensure the continuing administration of the government of the Islands. He shall discharge his functions in consultation with the representative institutions in the Islands which have been developed in accordance with the terms of Article 73 of the Charter of the United Nations, with the exception that one representative from the Argentine population normally resident on the Islands shall be appointed by the Administrator to each of the two institutions. The Administrator shall exercise his powers in accordance with the terms of this Agreement and in conformity with the laws and practices traditionally obtaining in the Islands.

(4)   The United Nations Administrator shall verify the withdrawal of all armed forces from the Islands, and shall devise an effective method of ensuring their non-reintroduction.

(5)   The United Nations Administrator shall have such staff as may be agreed by Argentina and the United Kingdom to be necessary for the performance of his functions under this Agreement.

(6)   Each Party may have no more than three observers in the Islands.

Article 7
Except as may be otherwise agreed between them, the Parties shall, during the currency of this Agreement, reactivate the Exchange of Notes of 5 August 1971, together with the Joint Statement on Communications between the Islands and the Argentine

mainland referred to therein. The Parties shall accordingly take appropriate steps to establish a special consultative committee to carry out the functions entrusted to the Special Consultative Committee referred to in the Joint Statement.

Article 8

The Parties undertake to enter into negotiations in good faith under the auspices of the Secretary-General of the United Nations for the peaceful settlement of their dispute and to seek, with a sense of urgency, the completion of these negotiations by 31 December 1982. These negotiations shall be initiated without prejudice to the rights, claims or positions of the Parties and without prejudgment of the outcome.

Article 9

This Interim Agreement shall enter into force on signature and shall remain in force until a definitive Agreement about the future of the Islands has been reached and implemented by the Parties. The Secretary-General will immediately communicate its text to the Security Council and register it in accordance with Article 102 of the Charter of the United Nations.

21. The Falkland Islands: Negotiations for a Settlement. British Government paper of 20 May 1982

Argentine Aggression

1.   It is now almost seven weeks since Argentina invaded the Falkland Islands. This unlawful use of force in unprovoked aggression threatened not only to destroy the democratic way of life freely chosen by the Falkland Islanders but also the basis on which international order rests. The invasion was also a singular act of bad faith: it took place when Britain and Argentina were engaged in negotiations in accordance with requests from the United Nations.

2.   On 1 April the President of the United Nations Security Council had formally appealed to Argentina not to invade the Falkland Islands. Yet on 2 April Argentina invaded. On 3 April, the United Nations Security Council passed its mandatory resolution 502, demanding a cessation of hostilities and an immediate withdrawal of all Argentine forces from the Islands. The same day, Argentina took South Georgia. In the ensuing weeks she has shown no sign of complying with the Security Council Resolution: on the contrary, she has continued a massive build-up of the occupying forces on the Falkland Islands. There could hardly be a clearer demonstration of disregard for international law and for the United Nations itself.

The British Response

3.   Britain need have done nothing more than rest on the mandatory resolution of the Security Council. Indeed Britain's inherent right of self-defence under Article 51 of the United Nations Charter would have justified the Government in adopting a purely military policy for ending the crisis. But in pursuit of a peaceful settlement, Britain adopted a policy, frequently explained by the Government in Parliament, of building up pressure on Argentina. Military pressure was exerted by the rapid assembly and dispatch of the British naval task force. Diplomatic pressure, first expressed in Security Council resolution 502, was built up by the clear statements of condemnation of Argentine aggression which were made by many countries across the world. It was widely recognised that aggression could not be allowed to stand, since otherwise international peace and order would be dangerously prejudiced in many regions. The members of the European Community, Australia, New Zealand, Canada and Norway joined Britain in rapidly imposing economic measures against Argentina, as did the United States a little later.

Efforts for a Negotiated Settlement

4.   Britain dedicated her maximum diplomatic efforts to the search for a negotiated solution, and the Government kept Parliament as fully informed as the confidentiality of difficult negotiations would allow. Efforts for an interim agreement to end the crisis were first undertaken by the United States Secretary of State, Mr Alexander Haig. His ideas for an interim agreement were discussed repeatedly with Argentina and Britain. The Government expressed their willingness to consider Mr Haig's final proposals, although they presented certain real difficulties. Argentina rejected them. The next stage

of negotiations was based on proposals originally advanced by President Belaúnde of Peru and modified in consultations between him and the United States Secretary of State. As the Foreign and Commonwealth Secretary informed Parliament on 7 May, Britain was willing to accept the final version of these proposals for an interim agreement. But Argentina rejected it.

5. Since then, the Secretary-General of the United Nations, Señor Pérez de Cuellar, has been conducting negotiations with Britain, represented by our Permanent Representative at the United Nations, Sir Anthony Parsons, and Argentina, represented by the Deputy Foreign Minister, Señor Ros. In these negotiations, as in earlier ones, Britain made repeated efforts to establish whether Argentina was willing to be sufficiently flexible to make a reasonable interim agreement possible. But it became increasingly clear that Argentina was not seeking an agreement but was playing for time in the negotiations in the hope of holding on to the fruits of aggression, with all that this would imply for the international rule of law. There was an important meeting of British ministers, attended by Sir Anthony Parsons and the British Ambassador in Washington, Sir Nicholas Henderson, on Sunday 16 May. On the following day, Sir Anthony Parsons returned to New York and handed to the United Nations Secretary-General two documents:

— a draft interim agreement between Britain and Argentina which set out the British position in full [see pp 58–61];

— a letter to the Secretary-General making clear the British position that the Falkland Islands dependencies were not covered by the draft interim agreement. . . .

6. Sir Anthony Parsons made clear to the Secretary-General that the draft agreement represented the furthest that Britain could go in the negotiations. He requested that the Secretary-General should give the draft to the Argentine Deputy Foreign Minister. The Secretary-General did this, and asked for a response within two days. Argentina's response, which the Government received on the evening of 19 May, represented a hardening of the Argentine position and amounted to a rejection of the British proposals.

Britain's Fundamental Principles in Negotiations

7. The Government's approach in all the negotiations has been based on important principles, which ministers have set out repeatedly in Parliament:

a. International Law. Argentina's unlawful aggression must end and Security Council resolution 502 must be implemented. Aggression must not be rewarded, or small countries across the world would feel threatened by neighbours with territorial ambitions.

b. Freedom. The Falkland Islanders are used to enjoying free institutions. The Executive and Legislative Councils were established with their agreement and functioned with their participation. Britain insisted that any interim administration in the Falkland Islands must involve democratically elected representatives of the Islanders, so as to enable the latter to continue to participate in the administration of their affairs and to ensure that they could express freely their wishes about the future of the Islands, in accordance with the principle of self-determination.

c. Sovereignty. Britain has no doubt of her sovereignty over the Falkland Islands, having administered them peacefully since 1833. Nevertheless, successive British Governments have been willing, without prejudice, to include the question of sovereignty in negotiations with Argentina about the future of the Falkland Islands. In the recent negotiations, the Government have been willing that an interim agreement should provide for new negotiations about the future of the Islands, which likewise could discuss sovereignty in good faith, so long as there was no prejudgment as to the outcome of negotiations.

8. Britain upheld these principles in the draft agreement which we presented on 17 May to the United Nations Secretary-General:

— The agreement provided for complete Argentine withdrawal from the Falkland Islands within 14 days, thus terminating the aggression and upholding international law.

— It provided that the Legislative and Executive Councils representing the Falkland Islanders would continue in existence and be consulted by the UN interim Administrator, thus maintaining the democratic structure of the Administration.

— It provided explicitly that the outcome of negotiations about the future of the Islands was not prejudged, thus safeguarding the British position on sovereignty.

9. In the Secretary-General's negotiations, Britain has insisted that the Falkland Islands dependencies should not be covered by an interim agreement to end the crisis. South Georgia and the South Sandwich Islands are geographically distant from the Falkland Islands themselves. They have no settled population. The British title to them, of which the Government have no doubt, does not derive from the Falkland Islands, and these territories have been treated as dependencies of the Falkland Islands only for reasons of administrative convenience.

10. Throughout the negotiations, Britain, while being firm on the essential principles, has been willing to negotiate on matters where these principles were not breached. In particular:

a. In return for Argentine withdrawal from a zone of 150 nautical miles radius around the Falkland Islands and an undertaking in the agreement that no forces would return, Britain was willing (Article 2(3)) to withdraw her task force from the zone and not return during the interim period. She proposed international verification (Article 6(4)) of the mutual withdrawal, in which the United Nations might have made use of surveillance aircraft from third countries.

b. Britain was willing that the exclusion zones (Article 3) declared by herself and Argentina, and the economic measures (Article 5) introduced during the present crisis, should be lifted from the moment of ceasefire, although these actions would give more comfort to Argentina than to Britain.

c. Britain was prepared to accept the appointment of a UN Administrator (Article 6(3)) to administer the government of the Falkland Islands. Britain wanted him to discharge his functions in consultation with the representative institutions in the Islands—the Legislative and Executive Councils—which have been developed in accordance with the terms of Article 73 of the UN Charter. (This makes clear that the interests of the inhabitants of non-self-governing territories are paramount and refs to the need to take due account of the political aspirations of the peoples.) It is inconceivable that Britain, or any other democratic country, could accept that her people should be deprived of their democratic rights. Britain was nevertheless willing to accept that one representative from the Argentine population of the Islands (some 30 people out of 1,800) should be added to each of the Councils. Additionally, Britain was willing to accept the presence of up to three Argentine observers on the Islands in the interim period.

d. Britain was willing (Article 7) to agree to re-establishment of communications, travel, transport, postage, etc, between the Falkland Islands and the Argentine mainland, on the basis existing before the invasion.

e. Britain was willing to enter into negotiations (Article 8) under the auspices of the UN Secretary-General for a peaceful settlement of the dispute with Argentina about the Falkland Islands and to seek the completion of these negotiations by the target date of 31 December 1982. Our position was that no outcome to the negotiations should be either excluded or predetermined.

11.   Argentina's final position in the negotiations speaks for itself. In particular:

a. Argentina insisted that South Georgia and the South Sandwich Islands be covered by the interim agreement. One effect of this would be that British forces would have to withdraw from the British territory of South Georgia.

b. Argentina wanted 30 days for the completion of the withdrawal of forces. She wanted all forces to return to their normal bases and areas of operation, thus requiring British forces to be enormously further away than Argentine ones.

c. Argentina wanted the Administration of the Islands to be exclusively the responsibility of the United Nations. There would have been Argentine and British observers. The Administration would have been free to appoint advisers from the population of the Islands, in equal numbers from the Argentine population and from the population of British origin. The flags of Britain and Argentina would have flown, together with that of the United Nations.

d. Argentina wanted free access for her nationals to the Islands, with respect *inter alia* to residence, work and property. Argentina also opposed a provision in the British draft agreement (end of Article 6(3)) about the UN Administrator exercising his powers in conformity with the laws and practices traditionally observed in the Islands. It was evident that Argentina hoped to change the nature of Falklands society and its demographic make-up in the interim period, and thus prejudge the future.

e. Argentina proposed a formula about negotiations on the future of the Islands which stated that they should be 'initiated' without prejudice to the rights and claims and positions of the two parties. Argentina would not accept an additional phrase stating also that the outcome would not be prejudged. Argentine leaders continued in public to say that Argentina insisted on having sovereignty. In the negotiations Argentina also resisted a provision in the British draft (beginning of Article 9) which would have ensured that the interim arrangements should stay in place until a definitive agreement about the future of the Islands could be implemented. Argentina's evident aim in resisting this was that, if no definitive agreement had been reached by the target date of 31 December 1982, the interim Administration would cease to exist and a vacuum be created which Argentina could hope to fill.

12. The present crisis was brought about by Argentina's unlawful act of aggression. In their subsequent attitude the Argentine Government showed that they had no respect either for democratic principles nor for the rule of law. Britain stands firmly for both.

22. The breakdown of negotiations: Speech by Mrs Margaret Thatcher opening the House of Commons' sixth debate on the Falklands crisis on 20 May 1982

Seven weeks ago today the Argentine Foreign Minister summoned the British Ambassador in Buenos Aires and informed him that the diplomatic channel was now closed. Later on that same day President Reagan appealed to President Galtieri not to invade the Falkland Islands. That appeal was rejected.

Ever since 2 April Argentina has continued to defy the mandatory resolution of the Security Council. During the past 24 hours the crisis over the Falkland Islands has moved into a new and even more serious phase.

On Monday of this week our ambassador to the United Nations handed to the Secretary-General our proposals for a peaceful settlement of the dispute. These proposals represented the limit to which the Government believe it was right to go. We made it clear to Señor Pérez de Cuellar that we expected the Argentine Government to give us a very rapid response to them.

By yesterday morning we had had a first indication of the Argentine reaction. It was not encouraging. By the evening we received their full response in writing. It was in effect a total rejection of the British proposals. Indeed, in many respects the Argentine reply went back to their position when they rejected Mr Haig's second set of proposals on 29 April. It retracted virtually all the movement that their representative had shown during the Secretary-General's efforts to find a negotiated settlement. I shall have some more to say about his efforts later.

The implications of the Argentine response are of the utmost gravity. This is why the Government decided to publish immediately the proposals that we had put to the Secretary-General and to give the House the earliest opportunity to consider them. These proposals were placed in the Vote Office earlier today. The Government believe that they represented a truly responsible effort to find a peaceful solution which both preserved the fundamental principles of our position and offered the opportunity to stop further loss of life in the South Atlantic.

We have reached this very serious situation because the Argentines clearly decided at the outset of the negotiations that they would cling to the spoils of invasion and occupation by thwarting at every turn all the attempts that have been made to solve the conflict by peaceful means. Ever since 2 April they have responded to the efforts to find a negotiated solution with obduracy and delay, deception and bad faith.

We have now been negotiating for six weeks. The House will recall the strenuous efforts made over an extended period by Secretary of State Haig. During that period my ministerial colleagues and I considered no fewer than four sets of proposals. Although these presented substantial difficulties, we did our best to help Mr Haig continue his mission, until Argentine rejection of his last proposals left him no alternative but to abandon his efforts.

The next stage of negotiations was based on proposals originally advanced by President Belaúnde of Peru and modified in consultations between him and Mr Haig. As my right hon. Friend the Secretary of State for Foreign and Commonwealth Affairs informed the House on 7 May, Britain was willing to accept these, the fifth set of proposals, for an interim settlement. They could have led to an almost immediate ceasefire. But again it was Argentina that rejected them.

I shall not take up the time of the House with a detailed description of those earlier proposals, partly because they belong to those who devised them, but, more importantly, because they are no longer on the negotiating table. Britain is not now committed to them.

Since 6 May, when it became clear that the United States-Peruvian proposals were not acceptable to Argentina, the United Nations Secretary-General, Señor Pérez de Cuellar, has been conducting negotiations with Britain and Argentina.

Following several rounds of discussions, the United Kingdom representative at the United Nations was summoned to London for consultation last Sunday. On Monday Sir Anthony Parsons returned to New York and presented to the Secretary-General a draft interim agreement between Britain and Argentina which set out the British position in full. He made it clear that the text represented the furthest that Britain could go in the negotiations. He requested that the draft should be transmitted to the Argentine representative and that he should be asked to convey his Government's response within two days.

Yesterday we received the Argentine Government's reply. It amounted to a rejection of our own proposals, and we have so informed the Secretary-General. This morning we have received proposals from the Secretary-General himself.

It will help the House to understand the present position if I now describe briefly these three sets of proposals.

I deal first with our own proposals. These preserve the fundamental principles which are the basis of the Government's position. Aggression must not be allowed to succeed. International law must be upheld. Sovereignty cannot be changed by invasion.

The liberty of the Falkland Islanders must be restored. For years they have been free to express their own wishes about how they want to be governed. They have had institutions of their own choosing. They have enjoyed self-determination. Why should they lose that freedom and exchange it for dictatorship?

Our proposals are contained in two documents. First, and mainly, there is a draft interim agreement between ourselves and Argentina. Secondly, there is a letter to the Secretary-General which makes it clear that the British Government do not regard the draft interim agreement as covering the dependencies of South Georgia and the South Sandwich Islands.[1]

I deal with the dependencies first. South Georgia and the South Sandwich Islands are geographically distant from the Falkland Islands themselves. They have no settled population. British title to them does not derive from the Falkland Islands but is separate. These territories have been treated as dependencies of the Falkland Islands only for reasons of administrative convenience. That is why they are outside the draft agreement.

The House has before it the draft agreement, and I turn now to its main features. Article 2 provides for the cessation of hostilities and the withdrawal of Argentine and British forces from the Islands and their surrounding waters within 14 days. At the end of the withdrawal British ships would be at least 150 nautical miles from the Islands. Withdrawal much beyond this would not have been reasonable, because the proximity of the Argentine mainland would have given their forces undue advantage.

---

[1] *This short letter, which forms Annex B of Document No 21, is not reproduced in this pamphlet.*

Withdrawal of the Argentine forces would be the most immediate and explicit sign that their Government's aggression had failed and that they were being made to give up what they had gained by force. It is the essential beginning of a peaceful settlement and the imperative of resolution 502.

Article 6 sets out the interim arrangements under which the Islands would be administered in the period between the cessation of hostilities and the conclusion of negotiations on the long-term future of the Islands.

In this interim period there would be a United Nations administrator, appointed by the Secretary-General and acceptable to Britain and the Argentine. He would be the officer administering the Government. Under clause 3 of this article he would exercise his powers in conformity with the laws and the practices traditionally obtained in the Islands. He would consult the Islands' representative institutions—that is the Legislative and Executive Councils through which the Islanders were governed until 2 April. There would be an addition to each of the two Councils of one representative of the 20 or 30 Argentines normally resident in the Islands. Their representatives would be nominated by the administrator.

The clause has been carefully drawn so that the interim administration cannot make changes in the law and customs of the Islanders that would prejudge the outcome of the negotiations on a long-term settlement.

This provision would not only go a long way to giving back to the Falklanders the way of life that they have always enjoyed, but would prevent an influx of Argentine settlers in the interim period whose residence would change the nature of society there and radically affect the future of the Islands. That would not have been a true interim administration. It would have been an instrument of change.

Clause 3 of this article thus fully safeguards the future of the Islands. Nothing in this interim administration would compromise the eventual status of the Falklands or the freedom which they have enjoyed for so long.

Clause 4 would require the administrator to verify the withdrawal of all forces from the Islands and to prevent their reintroduction. . . .

[*Replying to a question, Mrs Thatcher said that Britain had*] imported into this agreement Article 73 of the United Nations Charter, which refers to the paramountcy of the interests of the Islanders. During the long-term negotiations we shall closely consult the Islanders on their wishes and of course we believe in self-determination. That relates to the long-term negotiations. These articles deal with the interim administration, and I have been trying to make it clear that the interim administration must not have provisions within it which, in effect, pre-empt the outcome of the long-term negotiations.

I return to clause 4 of Article 6. We think it likely that the administrator will need to call upon the help of three or four countries other than ourselves and the Argentine to provide him with the necessary equipment and a small but effective force. The purpose of that is that if our troops leave the Islands we must have some way of guarding against another Argentine invasion. The safest way under these arrangements would be for the United Nations administrator to have a small United Nations force at his disposal, of the type I have described.

Articles 8 and 9 are also very important. They deal with negotiations between Britain and Argentina on the long-term future of the Islands.

The key sentence is the one which reads:

'These negotiations shall be initiated without prejudice to the rights, claims and positions of the parties and without prejudgment of the outcome.'

We should thus be free to take fully into account the wishes of the Islanders themselves. And Argentina would not be able to claim that the negotiations had to end with a conclusion that suited her. . . .

I have said that we do not prejudge the outcome. If the Islanders wished to go to Argentina, I believe that this country would uphold the wishes of the Islanders. After their experience I doubt very much whether that would be the wish of the Islanders. Indeed, I believe that they would recoil from it.

I return to Article 9. We have to recognise that the negotiations might be lengthy. That is why Article 9 provides that until the final agreement had been reached and implemented the interim agreement will remain in force.

Although this interim agreement does not restore things fully to what they were before the Argentine invasion, it is faithful to the fundamental principles that I outlined earlier. Had the Argentines accepted our proposals, we should have achieved the great prize of preventing further loss of life. It was with that in mind that we were prepared to make practical changes that were reasonable. But we were not prepared to compromise on principle.

I turn now to the Argentine response. This revived once again all the points which had been obstacles in earlier negotiations. The Argentine draft interim agreement applied not only to the Falklands but included South Georgia and the South Sandwich Islands as well. The Argentines demanded that all forces should withdraw, including our forces on South Georgia, and return to their normal bases and areas of operation. This was plainly calculated to put us at an enormous disadvantage.

They required that the interim administration should be the exclusive responsibility of the United Nations which should take over all executive, legislative, judicial and security functions in the Islands. They rejected any role for the Islands' democratic institutions.

They envisaged that the interim administration would appoint as advisers equal numbers of British and Argentine residents of the Islands, despite their huge disparity.

They required freedom of movement and equality of access with regard to residence, work and property for Argentine nationals on an equal basis with the Falkland Islanders. The junta's clear aim was to flood the Islands with its own nationals during the interim period, and thereby change the nature of Falklands society and so prejudge the future of the Islands.

With regard to negotiations for a long-term settlement, while pretending not to prejudice the outcome, the junta stipulated that the object was to comply not only with the Charter of the United Nations but with various resolutions of the General Assembly, from some of which the United Kingdom dissented on the grounds that they favoured Argentine sovereignty.

And if the period provided for the completion of the negotiation expired, the junta demanded that the General Assembly should determine the lines to which final agreement should conform. It was manifestly impossible for Britain to accept such demands.

Argentina began the crisis. Argentina has rejected proposal after proposal. One is bound to ask whether the junta has ever intended to seek a peaceful settlement or whether it has sought merely to confuse and prolong the negotiations while remaining in illegal possession of the Islands. I believe that if we had a dozen more negotiations the tactics and results would be the same. From the course of these negotiations and Argentina's persistent refusal to accept resolution 502 we are bound to conclude that its objective is procrastination and continuing occupation, leading eventually to sovereignty. . . .

As I said earlier, the Secretary-General has this morning put to us and to Argentina an aide-mémoire describing those issues where, in his opinion, agreement seems to exist and those on which differences remain.

The first group of issues—those where he believes there is a measure of agreement —would require further clarification, for on some points our interpretation would be different. The aide-mémoire states, for example, that Argentina would accept long-term negotiations without prejudgment of the outcome. This important phrase was, however, omitted from the Argentine response to our own proposals and is belied by a succession of statements from Buenos Aires.

Those points where, in the Secretary-General's judgment, differences remain include: first, aspects of the interim administration; secondly, the timetable for completion of negotiations and the related duration of the interim administration; thirdly, aspects of the mutual withdrawal of forces; and, fourthly, the geographic area to be covered. Señor Pérez de Cuellar has proposed formulations to cover some of those points.

The Secretary-General, to whose efforts I pay tribute, has a duty to continue to seek agreement. But, as our representative is telling him in New York, his paper differs in certain important respects from our position as presented to him on 17 May and which we then described as the furthest that we could go. Moreover, it differs fundamentally from the present Argentine position as communicated to us yesterday.

It is not a draft agreement, but, as the Secretary-General himself puts it, a number of formulations and suggestions. Some of his suggestions are the very ones which have already been rejected by the Argentine response to our own proposals. Even if they were acceptable to both parties as a basis for negotiation, that negotiation would take many days, if not weeks, to reach either success or failure.

We have been through this often before and each time we have been met with Argentine obduracy and procrastination. Argentina rejected our proposals. It is inconceivable that it would now genuinely accept those of the Secretary-General's ideas which closely resemble our own. . . .

This is the seventh set of proposals that we have considered. We have considered them carefully. Each time we have met with tactics the object of which is procrastination leading to continued occupation of the Islands. Because of the record on this matter we thought it best to put up our own specific draft interim agreement in writing so that our position was clear for the world to see and so that it was clear that we were not compromising fundamental principles, but that we were prepared to make some reasonable, practical suggestions if we could secure the prize of no further loss of life. Those proposals were rejected. They are no longer on the table.

. . . What is being considered is what is called an aide-mémoire, which is not a draft agreement, but a number of formulations and suggestions. The essence of those formulations and suggestions, where they are clear, is that they are those that have already been rejected by the Argentine response to our proposals. . . .

Even if we were prepared to negotiate on the basis of the aide-mémoire, we should first wish to see substantive Argentine comments on it, going beyond mere acceptance of it as a basis for negotiation. These are the points that we are making in our reply to the Secretary-General. At the same time, we are reminding him—as my right hon. Friends and I have repeatedly said to the House—that negotiations do not close any military options.

The gravity of the situation will be apparent to the House and the nation. Difficult days lie ahead, but Britain will face them in the conviction that our cause is just and in the knowledge that we have been doing everything reasonable to secure a negotiated settlement.

The principles that we are defending are fundamental to everything that this Parliament and this country stand for. They are the principles of democracy and the rule of law. Argentina invaded the Falkland Islands in violation of the rights of peoples to determine by whom and in what way they are governed. Its aggression was committed against a people who are used to enjoying full human rights and freedom. It was executed by a Government with a notorious record in suspending and violating those same rights.

Britain has a responsibility towards the Islanders to restore their democratic way of life. She has a duty to the whole world to show that aggression will not succeed and to uphold the cause of freedom.

23. United Nations' efforts to secure a diplomatic solution: Statement to the Security Council on 21 May 1982 by the Secretary-General of the United Nations, Señor Pérez de Cuellar

Mr President, I felt it my duty to inform you yesterday evening that my efforts to facilitate an agreement between the Republic of Argentina and the United Kingdom . . . initiated in pursuance of my responsibilities as Secretary-General, did not offer the . . . prospect of bringing an end to the crisis. The armed conflict persists and threatens to grow worse. In these grave circumstances, I wish to give the Council an account of the actions I have taken in pursuit of the objectives of Security Council resolution 502.

Following the adoption of that resolution, I continued my contacts with the parties and with the President of the Security Council concerning the situation. The views which I expressed were based on the Charter and on resolution 502, the implementation of which I repeatedly urged. I also made arrangements for contingency planning within the Secretariat, so that the United Nations could be in a position to implement effectively any responsibilities which might be entrusted to it.

As long as the efforts of the Government of the United States to facilitate a peaceful solution of the dispute in the context of the Council's resolution were under way, I voiced the hope that they would succeed, and I expressed the view that nothing should be done to interfere with that delicate process. At the same time, I affirmed my readiness to do all I could to be of assistance in achieving a peaceful solution.

In separate meetings on 19 April with the Permanent Representatives of Argentina and of the United Kingdom and also with the Permanent Representative of the United States, I outlined the assistance that the United Nations could render, if requested, in pursuance of any understanding or agreement that the parties might reach consistent with resolution 502. I stated that, for example, a small presence of United Nations civilian and military observers could be used to supervise any agreed withdrawal of armed forces and civilian personnel as well as any interim administrative arrangements. A United Nations 'umbrella' for such arrangements could also be provided, as could a United Nations temporary administration. I indicated that any arrangements of this kind would require the prior authorisation of the Security Council, that, as a practical matter, they would presuppose the consent of the parties, and that such arrangements were mentioned without prejudice to the possibility of other types of action that the Security Council might decide upon. An informal note was given to the Permanent Representatives summarising these ideas. Meanwhile, in connection with these ideas, detailed plans were developed as part of the contingency planning I have mentioned which could be made available to the parties at the appropriate time on the understanding that implementation would require a decision of the Security Council.

On 30 April, I met at United Nations Headquarters with Señor Nicanor Costa Mendez, Minister for Foreign Affairs and Worship of the Republic of Argentina. Later that day, I received a letter from Alexander Haig, Secretary of State of the United States of America, which provided information on the American proposal which had been presented to the parties and a statement of the position taken by the United States in the light of the existing situation.

In separate meetings on 2 May with the Secretary of State for Foreign and Commonwealth Affairs of the United Kingdom, Mr Francis Pym, and with the Permanent Representative of Argentina, I handed over an aide-mémoire in which I expressed my deep concern over the grave situation and emphasised my conviction that the United Nations had a most serious responsibility under the Charter urgently to restore peace and to promote a just and lasting settlement. I stated that the implementation of resolution 502 was imperative.

In my aide-mémoire, I suggested that the two Governments agree to take simultaneously the following steps which were conceived as provisional measures without prejudice to the rights, claims or position of the parties concerned. I proposed specifically that at a specific time:

(a)   the Argentine Government begin withdrawal of its troops from the Falkland Islands (Islas Malvinas) and the United Kingdom Government redeploy its naval forces and begin their withdrawal from the area of the Falkland Islands (Islas Malvinas), both Governments to complete their withdrawal by an agreed date;

(b)   both Governments commence negotiations to seek a diplomatic solution to their differences by an agreed target date;

(c)   both Governments rescind their respective announcements of blockades and exclusion zones and cease all hostile acts against each other;

(d)   both Governments terminate all economic sanctions;

(e)   transitional arrangements begin to come into effect under which the above steps would be supervised and interim administrative requirements met.

Reiterating my readiness to be of assistance, I recalled my conversations with the Permanent Representatives of the two parties on 19 April 1982 and I stated that practical arrangements for a United Nations role in a settlement could be completed expeditiously, subject to the consent of the parties and the decision of the Security Council.

On 5 and 6 May I received responses from the Government of Argentina and from the Government of the United Kingdom respectively. Both accepted the approach contained in the aide-mémoire as providing a basis or framework for an agreement that would bring the armed conflict to a halt and make possible a peaceful settlement. At the same time, the responses raised a number of points on which agreement was needed.

On 7 May the Under-Secretary for Foreign Affairs of Argentina, Señor Enrique Ros, arrived in New York to represent Argentina in the exchanges. Since that date, I have had some 30 separate meetings with the two sides with the purpose of assisting them in reaching an agreement along the lines suggested in my aide-mémoire of 2 May 1982. The intention was to develop the ideas spelled out in my aide-mémoire with a view to defining point by point the elements of a mutually acceptable text.

In my judgment, essential agreement was obtained, towards the end of last week, on the following points:

1.   The agreement sought would be interim in nature and would be without prejudice to the rights, claims or position of the parties concerned.

2.   The agreement would cover: (a) a ceasefire, (b) the mutual withdrawal of forces, (c) the termination of exclusion zones and of economic measures instituted in connec-

tion with the conflict, (d) the interim administration of the territory, and (e) negotiations on a peaceful settlement of their dispute.

3. The initiation of these various parts of an agreement would be simultaneous.

4. Withdrawal of forces would be phased and would be under the supervision of United Nations observers.

5. The interim administration of the territory would be under the authority of the United Nations. The United Nations flag would be flown. Argentina and the United Kingdom would establish small liaison offices, on which their respective flags could be flown.

6. The parties would enter into negotiations in good faith under the auspices of the Secretary-General of the United Nations for the peaceful settlement of their dispute and would seek, with a sense of urgency, the completion of these negotiations by 31 December 1982, taking into account the Charter of the United Nations and the relevant resolutions of the General Assembly. These negotiations would be initiated without prejudice to the rights, claims or position of the parties and without prejudging the outcome. The negotiations would be held in New York or its vicinity.

The crucial differences that remained concerned the following points, on which various options were being considered, at my suggestion:

1. Certain aspects of the interim administration of the territory.

2. Provisions for the extension of the time-frame for completion of negotiations and the related duration of the interim administration.

3. Certain aspects of mutual withdrawal of forces.

4. The geographic area to be covered by the terms of the interim agreement.

On 17 May the British Permanent Representative delivered to me the draft of an interim agreement on the Falkland Islands (Islas Malvinas) dispute which I transmitted to the Argentine Under-Secretary for Foreign Affairs on the same day. During the night of 18–19 May I received the text of an Argentine draft of such an interim agreement, which I promptly made available to the British side.

On studying these texts it was apparent that they did not reflect the progress which had, in my view, been achieved in the previous exchanges and that the differences on the four points remained.

On 19 May I spoke by telephone with President Galtieri and Prime Minister Thatcher to express my concern and suggest certain specific ideas which might assist the parties at this critical stage. Both agreed to give them consideration. I subsequently presented to the two sides on the same day a further aide-mémoire listing, as I have just done for the Council, the points on which I felt essential agreement had been reached and the four crucial questions which remained unresolved. I pointed out that the extent of agreement was, in my opinion, substantial and important—so much so that, if it were incorporated in the text of an interim agreement, the requirements of Security Council resolution 502 would be met. I expressed my deep concern, however, that unless the remaining points were resolved in the very immediate future, all that had been accomplished would be lost and the prospects for the early restoration of peace frustrated.

In the desire to be of assistance to the parties in the urgent requirement of overcoming these differences, I also included suggestions and formulations in my aide-mémoire of 19 May which might satisfactorily meet their preoccupations on the four important issues still unresolved, without prejudice to the rights, claims or position of either.

It remains my belief that an agreement along the lines developed in the exchanges over the past two weeks, incorporating the approaches suggested in my aide-mémoire of 19 May, could restore peace in the South Atlantic and open the way for an enduring solution of the long-standing dispute between two member states. By yesterday evening, however, the necessary accommodations had not been made. I concluded that, in the light of the Security Council's responsibilities under the Charter for the preservation of peace, I must urgently inform you, Mr President, of my appraisal of the situation. I did so at nine o'clock last night.

I would like to express appreciation for the important support that the Security Council has given to my efforts and for the understanding shown by the Council members as the exchanges with the parties have been under way. I would reiterate my personal commitment to be of assistance in every way toward the lasting resolution of this problem.

The prospect which faces us is one of destruction, continuing conflict and, above all, the loss of many, many young lives. Efforts must continue to find the means of avoiding this and restoring peace. There is no other course.

24. Statement to the Security Council on 21 May 1982 by Sir Anthony Parsons explaining the basic principles underlying Britain's policy

I should like to thank the Secretary-General for the account of the recent negotiations which he has just given. During the long and difficult negotiations, no one could have tried harder to bring about agreement than did the Secretary-General. My Government has complete faith in his ability and in his integrity. It is not through want of skill or trying that he has not succeeded. . . .

[*After describing the events which led up to the Security Council's adoption of resolution 502, Sir Anthony continued saying that*] . . . In the succeeding days, Argentina did not explicitly reject this resolution, no doubt for the very good reason that, as it was a mandatory resolution under Article 40 of the Charter—as was made clear at the time—it was not open to Argentina to purport to reject it. However, Argentina rejected the resolution in practice. Instead of withdrawing, Argentina reinforced its armed forces on the Falkland Islands. It imposed military government in the Islands in place of the previous democratic Government under which the British people of the Islands had lived peacefully in British territory for a century and a half. Argentina was bent on consolidating its grip on the Islands. In this situation, the United Kingdom had no choice but to exercise our inherent right of self-defence under Article 51 of the Charter. We have meticulously informed the President of the Council of every step we were taking in this regard. Possession of South Georgia was quickly recovered, with little resistance and only one casualty, on 22 April. But, 48 days after the adoption of resolution 502, Argentina remains in occupation of the Falkland Islands.

My Government could have stood from the outset on a position of absolute legitimacy—namely, that the aggressor must withdraw, that the *status quo ante* be restored, and that the diplomatic negotiations, which had been so rudely interrupted by the invasion, be resumed at the point at which they had been broken off.

However, in its strong desire for a peaceful solution, my Government was prepared to negotiate and, indeed, to show flexibility in these negotiations. Such negotiations were first undertaken through the good offices of the Secretary of State of the United States of America; thereafter through the President of Peru. The warmest tributes are due to both for their tireless efforts. In particular, I believe that Secretary Haig must have set an unbreakable record of shuttle diplomacy, in terms of time and distance covered. Even after their efforts had failed to produce results, my Government did not adopt the posture that no negotiations were possible, nor that diplomatic channels had been closed by Argentina's actions. Far from it. We welcomed the good offices of the Secretary-General on the basis of the broad range of ideas which he had presented to my Foreign Secretary, Mr Francis Pym. Tragically, the Secretary-General felt obliged to report on 20 May that his efforts had failed to produce the desired outcome.

Before reverting to the specific question of the latest round of negotiations, I should like to set out some basic principles.

The first one is peaceful settlement. It is clear that the Argentine invasions were violations of the third paragraph of Article 2 of the Charter—the fundamental principle of peaceful settlement [*see p 94*]. Both Argentina and the United Kingdom had long accepted that a dispute existed concerning sovereignty over the Falklands. The General Assembly had also accepted this. Instead of continuing to seek a peaceful settlement, on 2 and 3 April Argentina sought a military settlement. On 1 April the Argentine

Foreign Minister had expressly closed the diplomatic channels. These actions were contrary to a fundamental principle governing international relations, something which demands the severest censure from the international community. Even those who have a different view of the sovereignty question from my own must surely agree that Argentina, by using force, violated the fundamental obligation on all States to seek peaceful solutions to their differences. Argentina thus violated Article 2(3) and Article 37 of the Charter.

I turn now to the non-use of force. The Argentine invasion was carried out by the use of force against the entirely peaceful population of the Falkland Islands, people who had threatened no one at any time. There was no question of self-defence by Argentina. It is clear, therefore, that the Argentine action was also contrary to the fourth paragraph of Article 2 of the Charter. This is the obligation to:

'refrain ... from the ... use of force ... in any ... manner inconsistent with the Purposes of the United Nations'.

I need hardly remind this Council that the very first purpose of the United Nations is:

'. . . to bring about by peaceful means . . . settlement of international disputes . . .'. (*Article 1(1)*.)

Argentina was thus in breach of the Charter when on 2 April it began using force to try to settle the difference that existed between it and the United Kingdom over the Falkland Islands. Indeed, by its first use of armed force, Argentina committed an act of aggression within the meaning of the definition suggested by the General Assembly in resolution 3314 (XXIX). In his statement to this Council on 3 April, the Foreign Minister of Argentina attempted to advance a dangerous doctrine that the Charter in some unspecified way did not apply in the present situation because the problem arose before 1945. Quite clearly, there is absolutely no foundation in the Charter for such a dangerous doctrine. The Charter applies to everything in international relations which is happening in 1982: the roots of many problems under consideration by the United Nations stretch back years, decades, centuries before the Charter was adopted in 1945. Moreover, the Argentine action was clearly contrary to the rules of general international law prohibiting the use of force to settle problems—rules which exist alongside the Charter. The rules of international law do not contain an exception for old, pre-1945 differences between States.

Having established that the Argentine use of force was illegal, because it violated both paragraph 3 and paragraph 4 of Article 2 of the Charter, it follows that the military occupation of the Falkland Islands was and is also illegal. This was made clear by the Declaration on Friendly Relations, which was adopted by way of consensus in 1970 and which includes the following proposition:

'The territory of a State shall not be the object of military occupation resulting from the use of force in contravention of the provisions of the Charter.'

As if that were not enough, the continued Argentine occupation is also clearly contrary to operative paragraph 2 of Security Council resolution 502.

A word on self-defence. The situation facing the British Government is the following. British territory has been invaded by Argentine armed forces. British nationals are being subjected to both military occupation and military government against their freely expressed wishes. Argentina is using force day by day to occupy British territory and to subjugate the Falkland Islanders. Resolution 502 has proved insufficient to bring about withdrawal. Nothing could be clearer, against that background, than that the United Kingdom is fully entitled to take measures in exercise of its inherent right of self-defence, recognised by Article 51 of the Charter. If the Charter were otherwise, it would be a licence for the aggressor and a trap for the victim of aggression. The first use of force to settle disputes, to seize territory and to subjugate peoples is something which the Charter was intended to prevent.

I turn to the question of self-determination for the people of non-self-governing territories. The Charter is based on the principle of equal rights and self-determination of peoples. This is Article 1 (2). The common Article 1 of the two Covenents on Civil and Political Rights and on Economic, Social and Cultural Rights states clearly that 'all peoples have the right to self-determination'. Neither the Charter nor the Covenants attempt to lay down exceptions. In accordance with Article 73 of the Charter, the Declaration regarding Non-Self-Governing Territories, the principle is recognised that the interests of the inhabitants of territories such as the Falkland Islands are 'paramount'. At the same time, the inhabitants are 'within the system of international peace and security established by the present Charter'. In other words, the provisions about peaceful settlement and the non-use of force to which I have referred apply equally to non-self-governing territories. Article 73 speaks of development of self-government and the progressive development of free political institutions. It is institutions of this nature which the Falkland Islanders have long enjoyed. Indeed, it makes a mockery of the right to self-determination for Argentina to attempt to replace a democratic government and democratically elected bodies in the Falkland Islands with a military dictatorship. It adds insult to injury when this military dictatorship attempts, as it is doing, to change the way of life of the Falkland Islanders, to bring in settlers, to buy up land, to impose the Spanish language, to change the curricula in the schools and so on. All this is quite clearly contrary to the right of self-determination protected by the Charter. Indeed, it smacks of colonialism by Argentina.

It is grotesque for Argentina to criticise the system of government in the Falklands as colonial. We have heard about 'the need to remove all vestiges of colonialism from the Americas'. But the system of government has been endorsed by the people of the Falkland Islands in free and fair elections. What right have the leaders of Argentina to impose their form of military dictatorship on an entirely different people, who know democracy and cherish liberty? It will not have escaped notice that Argentina has not ratified either of the two Covenants on Human Rights, whereas the United Kingdom has ratified both and has done so on behalf of the Falkland Islands.

The United Nations has accepted since 1945 that the Falklands are a non-self-governing territory and that the United Kingdom is the administering authority. We have co-operated with the Committee of 24, which has reviewed the situation in the Falklands every year, annually. Last year the General Assembly asked the Committee to keep the situation under review and to report to the thirty-seventh session. We have fulfilled our obligations under Article 73. We have introduced political advances—a Legislative Council and an Executive Council, both with elected members. We are not prepared to turn back the clock and see those bodies abolished. It has been said, but not on any evidence, that the people of the Falklands are a transient, expatriate population. That is untrue. The census results show the lie. The Falkland Islanders have been in the Falkland Islands as long as, or longer than, most Argentine families have been in Argentina. They are an entirely separate people with a different language, culture and way of life from those of the people of Argentina.

The people of the Falklands have as much right to continue to live in the Falklands as the people of Argentina have the right to live in Argentina. Both peoples have the right to live under their own systems of government. Argentina has no right to deny the right of self-defence to the people of the Falkland Islands. Nor does it have the right to decide that Article 73 of the Charter no longer applies to them when it has so applied ever since 1945.

Argentina claims sovereignty on the basis of eighteenth- and early nineteenth-century history. Argentina's claim is not strengthened by anything that has happened since 1833. The United Kingdom has sovereignty on the basis of eighteenth-, nineteenth- and twentieth-century history; on the basis of the nationality of the population; on the basis of the freely chosen wishes of the people; and on the basis of what they have achieved in the territory.

When the press publishes pictures of houses, schools and churches in Stanley, these are houses, schools and churches which the Falkland Islanders—not General Menendez's forces—have built. The whole town of Stanley has been built since 1833. I could go on giving examples. But the message is clear. The Falkland Islanders have every right to the Islands and have every interest in being allowed to go back to their former way of life as soon as possible. Sovereignty is in dispute, but the people are not. It is not a case of two communities sharing the same territory.

I now come to the negotiations themselves—that is to say, the negotiations which have been taking place over the past ten days or so under the good offices of the Secretary-General. Throughout this period, as was the case during the previous negotiations, initiated by Secretary Haig and President Belaúnde, the British Government has exerted itself with the utmost good faith and the strongest sense of urgency. The discussions under the Secretary-General's auspices have been perhaps the most intensive and unremitting negotiations in which I have ever participated.

In the light of the progress which we hoped had been made, I was called back to London last weekend in order to take stock of the situation with my Government at the highest level. On my return on 17 May, I gave to the Secretary-General the final position of my Government in the form of a draft interim agreement, the text of which was released to the House of Commons yesterday and which has been published in full in *The New York Times* today [*see p 59*]. The position was, in the carefully considered judgment of my Government, the furthest point to which we could go in terms of flexibility without compromising principles which we are not prepared to abandon.

Let me illustrate what I mean by that. At the outset, I said that there would be a legitimate attitude for my Government—the total withdrawal of the aggressor, the restoration of the *status quo ante* and the resumption of the diplomatic negotiations which had been broken off. Now, we had reached a position by 17 May when we were prepared to contemplate much more than that. We were prepared to contemplate parallel withdrawal—parallel mutual withdrawal—not that the invader should withdraw first. We were prepared to contemplate this under United Nations supervision. We were prepared to contemplate a short interim period under United Nations administration in order to enable diplomatic negotiations to go forward for a definitive settlement of the problem. Although we insisted that the democratic institutions on the Islands should remain during the interim period, we were prepared to accept Argentine representation in these institutions disproportionate to the size of the Argentine community. We were prepared to accept an official Argentine observer during the interim period. I do not think that these points I have made demonstrate rigidity or inflexibility.

As my Foreign Secretary informed the House of Commons yesterday—I am paraphrasing his words—our first requirement has been to secure the withdrawal of Argentine forces, which was demanded as a matter of mandatory obligation by Security Council resolution 502. The second has been to establish a ceasefire to avoid further loss of life as soon as withdrawal could be agreed. The third has been to make satisfactory provision for the democratic administration of the Islands in any interim arrangements that might prove necessary. The fourth has been to ensure that the negotiations with Argentina over the future of the Islands should include terms of reference to make certain that these negotiations should not be such as to predetermine or to prejudge the outcome, whether on sovereignty or on other matters. The Foreign Secretary made clear in this connection that we remained prepared to negotiate with Argentina about the long-term future of the Islands. We would be ready to discuss anything which either side might wish to put forward, subject to the outcome of the negotiations being in no way predetermined or prejudged in advance. As members of the Council will see from study of our draft agreement and from what I have just said, we have stood firm where we have had to and we have shown flexibility where we could.

I regret to have to inform you, Mr President, and through you the members of the Council, that the response of the Government of Argentina to our proposals was wholly unsatisfactory. We had no choice but to regard this response, as had been the case in the previous rounds of negotiations, as a further attempt to procrastinate in order to enable Argentina to consolidate its hold on what it had seized by force. Specifically, the Argentine Government insisted on including South Georgia and the South Sandwich Islands in the agreement. This was unacceptable to us: these islands have nothing to do with our difference over the Falklands. They are nearly 1,000 miles away. They do not comprise an archipelago. They were administered from the Falklands only as a matter of convenience. They are uninhabited. Our title to them rests on totally different grounds to our title to the Falklands. Furthermore, the Government of Argentina insisted on an unequal process of withdrawal of forces which my Government could not accept. The Government of Argentina rejected the continuation in being during the interim period of the democratic institutions in the Islands which have been developed over the years in accordance with our obligations under Article 73 of the Charter. Argentina was only prepared to entertain the possibility that 'persons' who are members of the population of British origin and Argentine residents in the Islands, in equal numbers, might be appointed as 'advisers' by the United Nations interim administration. This was not only wholly unacceptable to us in concept, as it involved the dismantling of the democratic institutions to which I have referred, but the idea of parity in numbers of 'advisers' between a population of about 30 and a population of about 1,800 was ludicrous. Argentina required freedom of access with respect to residents and property during the interim period. This would have enabled it fundamentally to change the demographic status of the Islands during a short interim administration, clearly an unacceptable proposition. The Argentine formulation on how and when and by what means the negotiations should be concluded was also totally unacceptable to my Government. There was equally no assurance, contrary to what we had previously been led to believe, that Argentina had agreed to language which would leave it beyond doubt that the outcome of the negotiations should not be prejudged at the outset.

That is not an exhaustive list, but it is enough to demonstrate the justice of my Government's conclusion that the Argentine response amounted to a comprehensive rejection of our proposals.

The Secretary-General made a laudable last-minute attempt to see if the wide gulf between the parties could be bridged. My Government did not reject that initiative by the Secretary-General. I commented to him on the telephone yesterday, as my Prime Minister informed the House of Commons the same afternoon, that we appreciated the positive aspects in his initiative. I had to tell him that it differed in important respects from our final position and that, even if acceptable to both sides as a basis for negotiation, it would take days, if not weeks, to know whether success could be achieved. I told the Secretary-General that, before commenting in detail on his ideas, we should first need to see comprehensive comments from the Argentine side on every single point in them. The gulf was so wide between our final position and the response of the Government of Argentina that it would have been fruitless to continue unless we could have been certain that the Argentine reaction comprised a fundamental change of position and major movement towards positions which my Government could accept. No such reaction had been received by last night.

I also made clear to the Secretary-General, as I had made clear throughout the negotiations and as I have equally made plain to all members of the Council in informal consultations, that, although my Government's mind would never be closed to any avenue which promised to bring about a peaceful solution to the present crisis, we could not in the meantime allow ourselves to be in any way inhibited from carrying out military action in accordance with our inherent right of self-defence under Article 51 of the United Nations Charter. That remains our position today.

The British people are neither militaristic nor bellicose. Over the centuries many nations have made the mistake of interpreting our slowness to be aroused as weakness. This has always proved a profound mistake. We are not carried away by slogans or rhetoric, but we are implacably stubborn in defence of principles and the rights of peoples. In this instance, the principles of the peaceful settlement of disputes and of the non-use of force to settle political differences have been flagrantly breached by Argentine aggression. The rights of the people of the Falkland Islands have been trampled on by the invaders. We have reacted as we have always reacted to such challenges down the centuries of our history. Even so, we still hope and pray for a peaceful settlement, provided that it satisfies these principles and these rights.

25. The Falkland Islanders and self-determination: Statement to the Security Council on 25 May 1982 by Sir Anthony Parsons

In my main speech in this debate a few days ago I set out the full position of my Government on the present crisis up to that moment. I shall not weary the Council by going through all that again. My Government's views are plainly on the record. But I must take up some of the Council's time by responding to a number of the statements which have just been made by the Minister for Foreign Affairs of the Argentine Republic.

Several speakers, including the Minister for Foreign Affairs, have referred to the events of 1833. I should try to put them into proportion. I put out information about the history of the settlement of the Falkland Islands in my letter dated 28 April to the President of the Security Council and I attached to that letter a chronology of salient events. I shall now summarise those events briefly.

There were British settlements in the eighteenth century. There were also French and Spanish settlements. The latter were augmented by convicts. The Spanish settlements were abandoned in 1806 and the Islands were uninhabited for fully ten years before Buenos Aires became independent from Spain. The period from 1806 to 1833 was marked by some confusion. Many fishing vessels, as well as the United States naval ship *Lexington*, visited the Islands. Buenos Aires attempted to establish a colony—its word at the time—but other countries, including my own, did not accept [*its*] right . . .

It was for this reason that at the turn of the year 1832–33 a British ship visited the Islands. Port Stanley did not exist at the time. Captain Onslow of HMS *Clio* occupied Port Egmont. On reaching Soledad he found a detachment of 25 Buenos Ayrean soldiers and their schooner the *Sarandi*. A mutiny had previously occurred at Port Louis while the *Sarandi* was at sea and the commander of the Argentine schooner had placed the mutineers in irons aboard a British schooner after they had killed the Governor. At his request, they were taken to Buenos Aires. Most people elected to be repatriated: 18 were persuaded to stay behind. Not a shot was fired on either side. Captain Onslow re-asserted British sovereignty by raising the flag.

I have given this brief account in order to dispel any misapprehension about 1833. The events were nowhere near as dramatic as some other speakers have suggested. Those events brought to an end a period of uncertainty and were followed by 149 years of peace and prosperity, during which the only viable community that has ever existed on the Islands came into being.

The Foreign Minister of Argentina in his opening remarks talked of the outrage committed by the United Kingdom. So far as we are concerned, the outrage was committed by Argentina when, out of a clear blue sky, Argentine forces invaded the Falkland Islands at the beginning of April. This was recognised by the terms of Security Council resolution 502 which are only too familiar to members of the Council.

Why are we now in conflict? It is ludicrous to suggest that we are trying to create some new form of British empire in the South Atlantic. I cannot believe that anybody in their wildest imagination can credit this thesis. We are in conflict for very simple reasons. We are in conflict because, first, Argentina invaded the Islands and placed the community on the Islands under alien rule which they decidedly did not want and, secondly, because Argentina has consistently refused to carry out the unqualified demand to withdraw its forces, as demanded in resolution 502 of the Security Council.

The Foreign Minister referred at length to self-determination and referred to my country as the colonial power *par excellence*. It is true that we took the position in the 1960s that self-determination was a principle and not a right. However, in 1966 the two International Covenants—on Economic, Social and Cultural Rights, and on Civil and Political Rights—were adopted. These both state that:

'All peoples have the right of self-determination. By virtue of that right they freely determine their political status and freely pursue their economic, social and cultural development.'

The United Kingdom has ratified both these Covenants, which have entered into force. Furthermore, in 1970, the General Assembly adopted by consensus—that is, with the United Kingdom joining in the consensus—the Declaration on Principles of International Law concerning Friendly Relations and Co-operation among States in accordance with the Charter of the United Nations. This states:

'By virtue of the principle of equal rights and self-determination of peoples enshrined in the Charter of the United Nations, all peoples have the right freely to determine, without external interference, their political status . . .' etc.

Not only has my country endorsed the right to self-determination in the sense of the Charter, the Covenants and the friendly relations Declaration, but we have gone a great deal further to disprove the allegation that we are the colonial power *par excellence*. Since General Assembly resolution 1514 (XV)[1] was adopted at the end of 1960, we have brought to sovereign independence and membership of this Organisation no less than 28 states. We are proud of our record, and I think we have every right to be.

I turn now to the whole question of the people of the Falkland Islands. The Foreign Minister of Argentina has alleged that the application to the people of the Falkland Islands of self-determination is a travesty. This is simply not so. The people of the Falkland Islands are small in number—about 1,800—but as I have said on many previous occasions in this Council, this in no way at all detracts from their rights under international law, under the Charter of the United Nations, under Article 73 of that Charter. They are a community. They are a small community, but they are a peaceful community, they are a homogeneous community and they are a community which has developed democratic institutions over a period of a century.

I turn now to the recent round of negotiations which the Secretary-General conducted with such amazing diligence. We did not issue an ultimatum to the Government of Argentina. As I stated in my main statement to the Council a few days ago, we reached through very careful consideration at the highest level in London what my Government genuinely and carefully regarded as the furthest it could go in terms of flexibility without compromising principles which we were not in any circumstances prepared to abandon. One of those main principles was that, even in an interim period, the democratic, freely elected institutions of the people of the Falkland Islands could not be dismantled and set aside. To have agreed to this would have been a monstrous offence to our own beliefs, to our own responsibilities, to our responsibilities as a nation, to our responsibilities under the United Nations Charter.

---

[1] *The General Assembly resolution containing a declaration on the granting of independence to colonial peoples.*

All that the Government of Argentina was prepared to accept in this regard was that they might be used as advisers in a personal capacity by the interim administrator, provided that an equal number of citizens of Argentine origin could be similarly used. The Argentine community on the Islands amounts to approximately 30 people, the island community to approximately 1,800. Statistically that proposition was obviously totally unacceptable. Conceptually it was totally unacceptable because it would have led to the dismantlement of these institutions which have been developed and which have evolved since the nineteenth century. It is worth noting at this point that general elections were held in the Falkland Islands for the Councils as recently as October 1981. Were these simply to be set aside even during an interim period ?

I will not go into more detail about the nature of our reply and contrast it with the nature of the Argentine response. I have already done so, in great detail, in many ways. I would only say this: that throughout the seven weeks of negotiations my Government made many adjustments to our original position, in the sincere and heartfelt hope of reaching a peaceful solution. We reached a point where we believed that we could go no further without, as I have just said, the compromise of principles which we were not prepared to compromise.

When we received the response of the Government of Argentina it appeared to us to demonstrate no advance over its initial position at the outset of the negotiations outside the United Nations forum seven weeks previously. We had no choice but to regard it as a comprehensive rejection of our proposals.

The situation remains as it has remained ever since the beginning of April. The cause of the conflict is the Argentine invasion of the Falklands and Argentina's refusal to withdraw in accordance with the mandatory demand contained in Security Council resolution 502. The effect is the conflict which is causing all of us such grave concern. Remove the cause, the illegal Argentine presence on the Islands, and the effect will disappear. We have no other desire but to protect the rights under the Charter of the United Nations, under international law, of the Falkland Islanders, to redress the wrong which has been done, to demonstrate that political disputes cannot and must not be settled by the use of armed force, and to demonstrate beyond any shadow of doubt that aggression must not and cannot be allowed to pay.

26. Security Council Resolution 505 of 26 May 1982

The Security Council,

reaffirming its Resolution 502 (1982) of 3 April 1982:

noting with the deepest concern that the situation in the region of the Falkland Islands (Islas Malvinas) has seriously deteriorated:

having heard the statement made by the Secretary-General to the Security Council at its . . . meeting on 21 May 1982, as well as the statements in the debate of the representatives of Argentina and of the United Kingdom of Great Britain and Northern Ireland:

concerned to achieve as a matter of the greatest urgency a cessation of hostilities and an end to the present conflict between the armed forces of Argentina and of the United Kingdom of Great Britain and Northern Ireland:

1. expresses appreciation to the Secretary-General for the efforts which he has already made to bring about an agreement between the parties to ensure the implementation of Security Council Resolution 502 (1982), and thereby to restore peace in the region:

2. requests the Secretary-General, on the basis of the present resolution, to undertake a renewed mission of good offices bearing in mind Security Council Resolution 502 (1982) and the approach outlined in his statement of 21 May 1982:

3. urges the parties to the conflict to co-operate fully with the Secretary-General in his mission with a view to ending the present hostilities in and around the Falkland Islands (Islas Malvinas):

4. requests the Secretary-General to enter into contact immediately with the parties with a view to negotiating mutually acceptable terms for a ceasefire, including, if necessary, arrangements for the dispatch of United Nations observers to monitor compliance with the terms of the ceasefire:

5. requests the Secretary-General to submit an interim report to the Security Council as soon as possible and in any case not later than seven days after the adoption of this resolution.

27. Statement to the Security Council on 26 May 1982 by Sir Anthony Parsons pledging Britain's support for efforts to secure the implementation of Security Council resolution 502

I should first like to express the very heartfelt appreciation of my delegation to those non-aligned delegations which have worked so hard to produce a text of a resolution which has just commanded unanimity in the Council.

My delegation voted in favour of the resolution . . . because it contains a clear reaffirmation of Security Council resolution 502. It registers beyond doubt that the Secretary-General's efforts have been and will be concentrated on ensuring the implementation of Security Council resolution 502. This is the key to the return of peace to the region, which all of us so devoutly wish. In particular, this key lies in the second operative paragraph of that resolution, namely the unconditional demand for the immediate withdrawal of all Argentine forces from the Falkland Islands.

My delegation will certainly co-operate fully with the Secretary-General in his renewed mission. In the light of certain statements made by delegations in the debate and in explanation of vote this morning, I must make clear, so that there is absolutely no misunderstanding, that for our part the only acceptable condition for a ceasefire is that it should be unequivocally linked with an immediate commencement of Argentine withdrawal. The history of the past two months has done nothing to create British confidence in the Government of Argentina. First, Argentina invaded the Falkland Islands without warning while negotiations were still in progress and in defiance of the Security Council's appeal of 1 April. Secondly, we have exerted ourselves to the utmost in six rounds of negotiations for a peaceful settlement of the crisis brought about by the Argentine invasion. In every instance we have found at the end that we have travelled in a circle, or rather that we have never left the point of departure. Hence, a simple verbal agreement by Argentina to withdraw its forces would not be sufficient for a ceasefire. This must be on the basis of an Argentine commitment to practical and irrevocable arrangements for immediate withdrawal.

The Council should also be quite clear on another point. The situation has changed since the Secretary-General reported to the Council on 21 May. Operative paragraph 2 of Security Council resolution 502 is plainly stated. We are talking about Argentine withdrawal. We cannot now accept that Argentine withdrawal be linked in any way to parallel British withdrawal.

We do not minimise the difficulty of the Secretary-General's task but I would be the last to underestimate his great skill and devotion. If anyone can succeed in the task before him, it is our Secretary-General, and I should like again to assure the Council that my delegation will co-operate with him to the full.

I cannot conclude this statement without expressing a little surprise at the explanation of vote, or parts of it, just delivered by the representative of the Soviet Union. On 1 April the Soviet Union joined in the call by all members of the Security Council to Argentina and the United Kingdom to refrain from the use of force. On 2 April Argentina did use force. This was registered in Security Council resolution 502, which the Soviet Union did not oppose. I am still waiting to hear a word of condemnation of this first use of force from my colleague from the Soviet Union. He has adopted . . . a one-eyed stance this morning, not seeing the use of force by Argentina but focusing with one eye on the United Kingdom's actions in exercise of our right to self-defence.

Statement to the Security Council on 2 June 1982 by Sir Anthony Parsons explaining Britain's opposition to any call for an unconditional ceasefire

I pay tribute once again to the Secretary-General for the efforts he has made during the past few days to bring about the implementation of resolutions 502 and 505. The fact that it has not proved possible to negotiate mutually acceptable terms for a ceasefire is not in any way the fault of the Secretary-General. He has again displayed the highest qualities demanded of his office.

I have said before—but it cannot be repeated too often—that the current breach of the peace was caused by Argentina. It was Argentina that closed the diplomatic channel on 1 April. It was Argentina that remained silent in the face of the Security Council's appeal not to use force, later that same day, at the 2,345th meeting of this Council. It was Argentina which the next morning invaded the Falkland Islands. It was and is Argentina that has failed to comply with resolution 502, which demanded the immediate withdrawal of all Argentine troops. Far from withdrawing them, Argentina reinforced them.

It is the United Kingdom which was the victim of the Argentine act of aggression. It is the Falkland Islanders who have been the victims of the Argentine use of force to occupy the Islands. I do not propose now to dwell on the traumatic experiences the Islanders have suffered over the past two months. The reports so far are necessarily incomplete, but from those areas where Islanders have been able to talk freely of their experiences under Argentine occupation some very sombre and disturbing facts are beginning to emerge.

I have had occasion at previous meetings of this Council to set out the United Kingdom's position in detail and I shall not weary the Council by repeating all my arguments, which, I believe, effectively refuted some of the more extravagant distortions advanced today by the representative of Argentina. I must repeat once again that it was Argentina which first used force and began the present crisis. Everything we have done since has been in exercise of our inherent right of self-defence. We have never argued that the United Kingdom was assuming the task of executing the mandate from the Security Council. The true position is that, in the face of Argentina's flagrant and open violation of resolution 502, we have exercised our right of self-defence, for which no mandate of the Security Council is required by the terms of the Charter of the United Nations.

Our objectives have been clear: aggression must not be allowed to pay. Peoples must not be subjugated against their will. Peoples must enjoy the right to self-determination. Political problems must not be settled by armed force. These are principles which my Government has not been prepared to compromise. They have nothing to do with 'colonialism', 'imperialism' and outworn shibboleths of that kind. What conceivable reason could my country have for wishing to establish British or other military power in the South Atlantic? If we had had such extraordinary pretensions, I suggest to the Council that we would have kept a larger garrison than 40 Royal Marines on the Falklands before the Argentine invasion.

We have done everything in our power, short of compromising the principles I have set out, to bring about the peaceful implementation of the central element of Security Council resolution 502, namely, unconditional Argentine withdrawal from the Islands.

This has not so far proved possible, and we have been left with no choice but to defend these principles by other means. We have never broken off or interrupted negotiations. We have negotiated fully and in good faith throughout this long period.

I turn now to the recent negotiations for a ceasefire. These negotiations were held pursuant to paragraph 4 of resolution 505. As members of the Council will recall, this resolution reaffirmed resolution 502, by which the Council—as long ago now as 3 April—demanded the immediate withdrawal of all Argentine forces from the Falkland Islands. The United Kingdom's position was that it would welcome a ceasefire which was inseparably linked to the commencement of the withdrawal of Argentine forces and to the completion of their withdrawal within a fixed period. This position was based squarely on resolution 502.

The representative of Argentina has set out in full the responses of his Government during the past week. He has also purported to set out the positions of my Government. I do not intend to follow him down that particular road of controversy. The Secretary-General has maintained a unique confidentiality about the nature of his negotiations since the outset, and even in the face of the statement by the representative of Argentina, I do not intend to breach that confidence. I would only say this: that the explanation by the representative of Argentina makes clear, in my judgment, that if Argentine preconditions had been accepted they would have led us back into the morass of procrastination and evasion which my Government has experienced on the part of the Government of Argentina over the past two months of extremely intensive negotiation.

The plain fact is that until the Government of Argentina changes its position, it is clear that the conditions for a ceasefire do not exist. Against this background, the call by the representatives of Spain and Panama for an unconditional, immediate ceasefire is not acceptable to my delegation. A ceasefire which is not inseparably linked to an immediate Argentine withdrawal would not be consistent with resolution 502, because that resolution demands the immediate withdrawal of all Argentine forces from the Falkland Islands. The call for an unconditional ceasefire would leave Argentine forces in position.

As I indicated earlier, the United Kingdom is perfectly prepared for a ceasefire so long as it is inextricably linked to implementation of the demand in resolution 502 for Argentine withdrawal. We have no wish to inflict or to suffer further casualties. We are ready to discuss honourable arrangements for the departure of Argentine forces in accordance with resolution 502. But the Council's demand for withdrawal must be heeded. Because the call for a ceasefire contained in the draft resolution read out by the representative of Spain does not link that ceasefire with withdrawal, my delegation will be obliged to oppose it.

A resolution better fitted to the needs of the present situation would, I suggest, contain the following elements: a reaffirmation of resolutions 502 and 505 in all their parts; an expression of appreciation to the Secretary-General for his continuing efforts towards peace-making; a reiteration of the demand in resolution 502 for Argentine withdrawal; a call for a ceasefire which would come into effect as soon as watertight arrangements existed for Argentine withdrawal within a fixed period, in dignity and on an honourable basis. These arrangements would, as a practical matter, have to be agreed between the military commanders of the two sides in the Islands.

These are the essential elements of a ceasefire resolution which I commend to the Council. My delegation could support such a resolution.

In conclusion, at the risk of repeating myself, I should like to emphasise one thing. The objective of my Government is to set free the people of the Falkland Islands from Argentine occupation, which, by their own democratic decision, they never, never wanted. All we wish to do is to enable those people to resume their peaceful, harmless and inoffensive lives and to make up their own minds, in freedom and without constraint, regarding their long-term future. When we talk about security arrangements for the future, we are talking about security arrangements to shield the Islanders against any threat of renewed aggression. That is all.

29. Surrender of Argentine forces on the Falkland Islands: Statement by Mrs Margaret Thatcher in the House of Commons on 15 June 1982

... Early this morning in Port Stanley, 74 days after the Falkland Islands were invaded, General Moore accepted from General Menendez the surrender of all the Argentine forces in East and West Falkland together with their arms and equipment....

General Menendez has surrendered some 11,000 men in Port Stanley and some 2,000 in West Falkland. In addition, we had already captured and were holding elsewhere on the Islands 1,800 prisoners, making in all some 15,000 prisoners of war now in our hands. [*The total was later found to be just over 11,000—see p 14*].

The advance of our forces in the last few days is the culmination of a determined military effort to compel the Argentine Government to withdraw their forces from the Falkland Islands.

On the night of Friday 11 June, men of 42 and 45 Commandos and the 3rd Battalion the Parachute Regiment, supported by elements of the Royal Artillery and Royal Engineers, mounted an attack on Argentine positions on Mount Harriet, Two Sisters and Mount Longdon. They secured all their objectives, and during the next day consolidated their positions in the face of continuing resistance.

I regret to inform the House that five Royal Marines, 18 Paratroopers and two Royal Engineers lost their lives in those engagements. Their families are being informed. Seventy-two Marines and Paratroopers were wounded. We have no details of Argentine casualties. Hundreds of prisoners and large quantities of equipment were taken in these operations. The land operations were supported by Harrier attacks and naval gunfire from ships of the task force which made a major contribution to the success of our troops. In the course of the bombardment, however, HMS *Glamorgan* was hit by enemy fire. We now know that 13 of the crew died in this attack or are missing.

Throughout Sunday 13 June, the 3rd Commando Brigade maintained pressure on the enemy from its newly secured forward positions. Meanwhile, men of the 5th Infantry Brigade undertook reconnaissance missions in preparation for the next phase of the operations. HMS *Hermes* flew her one-thousandth Sea Harrier mission since leaving the United Kingdom.

The Argentines mounted two air raids that day. The first was turned back by Harriers of the task force before it could reach the Falklands. In the second raid A4 [*Skyhawk*] aircraft made an unsuccessful bombing run and one Mirage aircraft was shot down.

During the night of Sunday 13 June the second phase of the operations commenced. The 2nd Battalion the Parachute Regiment secured Wireless Ridge and the 2nd Battalion the Scots Guards took Tumbledown Mountain by first light on Monday 14 June. The 1st/7th Gurkhas advanced on Mount William, and the Welsh Guards on Sapper Hill. At 2 pm London time large numbers of Argentine troops were reported to be retreating from Mount William, Sapper Hill and Moody Brook in the direction of Port Stanley.

British forces pressed forward to the outskirts of Port Stanley. Large numbers of Argentines threw down their weapons and surrendered.

At 4 o'clock the Argentine garrison indicated its willingness to talk. Orders were given to our forces to fire only in self-defence. Shortly before 5 o'clock a white flag appeared over Port Stanley.

Initial contact was made with the enemy by radio. By midnight General Moore and

General Menendez were talking. The surrender of all the Argentine forces of East and West Falkland was agreed at 1 am today London time. Some of our forces are proceeding to West Falkland to organise the surrender of the Argentine forces there.

We are now tackling urgently the immense practical problems of dealing with the Argentine prisoners on the Islands. . . . We have already repatriated to Argentina almost 1,400 prisoners, and the further 15,000 now in our custody are substantially more than we had expected. With the help of the International Red Cross, we are taking urgent steps to safeguard these prisoners and hope to evacuate them as soon as possible from the Islands, in accordance with our responsibilities under the Geneva Convention. This is a formidable task.

We have today sent to the Argentine Government, through the Swiss Government, a message seeking confirmation that Argentina, like Britain, considers all hostilities between us in the South Atlantic—and not only on the Islands themselves—to be at an end. It is important that this should be established with clarity and without delay.

We must now bring life in the Islands back to normal as quickly as possible, despite the difficult conditions and the onset of the Antarctic winter. Mines must be removed; the water supply in Stanley is not working and there will be other urgent tasks of repair and reconstruction.

Mr Rex Hunt and members of the Islands council at present in this country will return as soon as possible. Mr Hunt will concentrate on civilian matters. General Moore will be responsible for military matters. They will in effect act as civil and military commissioners and will, of course, work in the closest co-operation.

After all that has been suffered it is too early to look much beyond the beginning of the return to normal life. In due course the Islanders will be able to consider and express their views about the future. When the time is right we can discuss with them ways of giving their elected representatives an expanded role in the government of the Islands. . . .

We shall uphold our commitment to the security of the Islands; if necessary we shall do this alone. But I do not exclude the possibility of associating other countries with their security. Our purpose is that the Falkland Islands should never again be a victim of unprovoked aggression.

Recognising the need for economic development, I have asked Lord Shackleton to update his 1976 report on the economic potential of the Islands. He has agreed to do this as a matter of urgency.[1] I am most grateful to him.

The House will join me, Mr Speaker, in expressing our deep sense of loss over those who have died, and our sorrow for their families. The final details will not become clear for a few days yet, but we know that some 250 British servicemen and civilians have been killed. They died that others may live in freedom and justice.

The battle of the Falklands was a remarkable military operation, boldly planned, bravely executed, and brilliantly accomplished. We owe an enormous debt to the British forces and to the Merchant Marine. We honour them all. They have been supported by a people united in defence of our way of life and of our sovereign territory.

---

[1] *Lord Shackleton's report,* Falkland Islands Economic Study 1982 *(Cmnd 8653, HMSO, £7·80, ISBN 0 10 186530 9), was published in September 1982.*

30. Repossession of Southern Thule: Letter sent to the President of the Security Council by Sir Anthony Parsons on 21 June 1982

... The South Sandwich Islands lie approximately 1,500 miles east-south-east of Cape Horn in the Antarctic Ocean, to the north of the Antarctic Treaty area. The Islands were discovered by a British national, Captain Cook, and British sovereignty was proclaimed in 1775, before which the Islands were *terra nullius*. The Islands have long been administered by the United Kingdom, which was accepted by Argentina until Argentina first advanced a claim to the Islands in 1937. In the 1940s and 1950s, the United Kingdom offered to refer the question of sovereignty over the Islands to the International Court of Justice but Argentina declined to accept the Court's jurisdiction.

In 1976, the United Kingdom became aware of the establishment of an Argentine station on Southern Thule for which no authorisation had been sought. Accordingly the United Kingdom protested at the time against these illegal actions and has subsequently maintained in protests to Argentina that this illegal presence was totally unacceptable.

On 2 April 1982, Argentina purported to proclaim 'the recovery of its national sovereignty' over the Falkland Islands, South Georgia and the South Sandwich Islands. This proclamation was brought to the attention of the Security Council by the representative of Argentina in his statement at . . . the meeting of the Security Council on 2 April 1982. At the same time, Argentina used armed force in order to invade the Falkland Islands and South Georgia while maintaining its illegal presence on Southern Thule.

. . . I now have the honour to report the recovery of possession of the South Sandwich Islands. The Argentine station comprised ten naval and one air force personnel. They formally surrendered on board HMS *Endurance* at 19.00 hours GMT on 20 June. At no time were any shots fired by British forces. This action was undertaken in exercise of the United Kingdom's inherent right of self-defence recognised by Article 51 of the Charter of the United Nations.

31. Extracts from the United Nations Charter

Article 1

The Purposes of the United Nations are:

1. To maintain international peace and security, and to that end: to take effective collective measures for the prevention and removal of threats to the peace, and for the suppression of acts of aggression or other breaches of the peace, and to bring about by peaceful means, and in conformity with the principles of justice and international law, adjustment or settlement of international disputes or situations which might lead to a breach of the peace;

2. To develop friendly relations among nations based on respect for the principle of equal rights and self-determination of peoples, and to take other appropriate measures to strengthen universal peace . . .

Article 2

The Organisation and its Members, in pursuit of the Purposes stated in Article 1, shall act in accordance with the following Principles.

1. The Organisation is based on the principle of the sovereign equality of all its Members.

2. All Members, in order to ensure to all of them the rights and benefits resulting from membership, shall fulfil in good faith the obligations assumed by them in accordance with the present Charter.

3. All Members shall settle their international disputes by peaceful means in such a manner that international peace and security, and justice, are not endangered.

4. All Members shall refrain in their international relations from the threat or use of force against the territorial integrity or political independence of any state, or in any other manner inconsistent with the Purposes of the United Nations.

5. All Members shall give the United Nations every assistance in any action it takes in accordance with the present Charter, and shall refrain from giving assistance to any state against which the United Nations is taking preventive or enforcement action.

Article 33

1. The parties to any dispute, the continuance of which is likely to endanger the maintenance of international peace and security, shall, first of all, seek a solution by negotiation, enquiry, mediation, conciliation, arbitration, judicial settlement, resort to regional agencies or arrangements, or other peaceful means of their own choice.

2. The Security Council shall, when it deems necessary, call upon the parties to settle their dispute by such means.

Article 51

Nothing in the present Charter shall impair the inherent right of individual or collective self-defence if an armed attack occurs against a Member of the United Nations, until the Security Council has taken measures necessary to maintain international peace and security. Measures taken by Members in the exercise of this right of self-defence shall be immediately reported to the Security Council and shall not in any way affect the authority and responsibility of the Security Council under the present Charter to take at any time such action as it deems necessary in order to maintain or restore international peace and security.

Article 73

Members of the United Nations which have or assume responsibilities for the administration of territories whose peoples have not yet attained a full measure of self-government recognise the principle that the interests of the inhabitants of these territories are paramount, and accept as a sacred trust the obligation to promote to the utmost, within the system of international peace and security established by the present Charter, the well-being of the inhabitants of these territories, and, to this end:

(a)   to ensure, with due respect for the culture of the peoples concerned, their political, economic, social, and educational advancement, their just treatment, and their protection against abuses;

(b)   to develop self-government, to take due account of the political aspirations of the peoples, and to assist them in the progressive development of their free political institutions, according to the particular circumstances of each territory and its peoples and their varying stages of advancement;

(c)   to further international peace and security;

(d)   to promote constructive measures of development, to encourage research and to co-operate with one another and, when and where appropriate, with specialised international bodies with a view to the practical achievement of the social, economic, and scientific purposes set forth in this Article; and

(e)   to transmit regularly to the Secretary-General for information purposes, subject to such limitation as security and constitutional considerations may require, statistical and other information of a technical nature relating to economic, social and educational conditions in the territories for which they are respectively responsible other than those territories to which Chapters XII and XIII apply.

Printed in England for Her Majesty's Stationery Office by Collins & Wilson Ltd., London and Andover
Dd 8299314   C25   12/82